To Frank:

I hope you enjoy reading my memoir, Normal Secrets.

Rosemarie and I look fondly on the trips you and your family have made to visit us in Florida. You have an amazing family!

Happy Reading and Best Wishes for the Future.

Walter F. Kern
April 3, 2017

Also by Walter F. Kern

Getting Started Riding a Motorcycle
50 Wild Motorcycle Tales
Motorcycle Haiku Poetry
Motorcycle Kick-Starts

Normal Secrets

A Search for Identity, Growth, Love, and Motorcycles

Walter F. Kern

a memoir

Dedicated to Susan Carol McKenna

Contents

Preface

This memoir is a departure from the motorcycle themes of my previous four books. For a long time I have been thinking how I might unveil secrets that my ancestors held tightly in the shadows. But would those secrets even be interesting to a general audience, I wondered. After all, I'm not a famous politician, business leader, rock star, or movie or television entertainer. I guess I've lived a life much like that of my readers, but it does have unusual twists and turns known only by a few family members. Many secrets revealed here were unknown to me until late in life. They had to be mined slowly from personal interviews, genealogical studies, public records, and some cutting-edge scientific laboratory work accomplished by worldwide experts. My story isn't complete yet, but I thought it was time at the age of 79 that I should attempt to put it down in a memoir.

A memoir is not supposed to be an autobiography of one's entire life; rather, it should focus on a few notable portions, including people and events that shaped the writer's life. I hope you will gain a better understanding of my life as I pursued it, not even knowing who I was, what I was searching for, who I would marry, how I would deal with adversity, and why I would come to be so intimately involved with, of all things, motorcycles. But my greater hope is that you will travel along with me on my journey and consider what you would have done at each decision point. Did I make the right choice? Did I make the wrong choice? Are you learning anything that might help you in your own journey? I sincerely hope that you will benefit from reading this memoir.

I've told some of my life stories to a few people, but I'm sure not many remember the details. This memoir sets down in print what significant events I remembered, what people were important to me, how I went about solving problems, and what I gave back to others. I was fortunate in that I took the time to write about some of my experiences—and published some—shortly after they occurred. These are also included in the memoir. Since these additional writings were done at different ages, I left them unedited to preserve both the way I was thinking at the time and how I put my words down on paper. Also, some of the people in my life sent me letters that I considered to be significant to the telling of this story. I have also used their exact words, unedited. Perhaps the pathway I traveled, using the mind to rise up and move forward to an uncertain future, will prompt readers to examine their own lives and, likewise, assist them in their own growth.

1. A Few Drops of Blood

Do nothing secretly;
for Time sees and hears all things,
and discloses all.

-- Sophocles

October 13, 1998

I was a bit nervous today, alone in the house, waiting to uncover a secret. I was seated in my family room on the white well-worn imitation leather couch. I was facing the front door and had my arms on a fold-up wooden TV tray. On the tray were a small piece of white cotton cloth and a set of instructions. The instructions (below) had arrived in an email from a researcher at Oxford University in England:

> (1) Spot a few drops of blood onto a piece of clean cloth.
> (2) Allow to dry in the air at room temperature.
> (3) Place in a paper envelope or between sheets of clean dry paper and store dry at room temperature.
> (4) When you have both samples, send them to us in the post.

When I first read the instructions a week ago, I was concerned when the first step said, "Spot a few drops of blood onto a piece of clean cloth." I had never even liked the sight of blood. Now I had been asked to cut myself intentionally. That was not going to happen! But I had to do it, I conceded, to find out the truth. Immediately, I thought of my first-born son, David, who had contracted type 1 diabetes at the age of 10. Now 36 years old and completely used to taking blood tests every day, he would be the one who could help me.

David had agreed to come over, but I hated the waiting. I already had waited a long time. I was now 60 years old, and I wasn't sure where I came from! I like to get things done and have always made to-do lists to help me keep getting things done. I don't like procrastinating even when it involves something I don't want to do. I leaned back on the couch, interleaving my fingers on the back of my head as I often do when taking a break. I inhaled deeply then let out an audible sigh.

While waiting for David, yet dreading his arrival, I thought about my past.

2. Bloomington-Normal

1938

I was born in Bloomington, Illinois, in 1938 and lived on East Beecher Street. When I was two years old, we moved to South Linden Street in Normal, Illinois.

Bloomington and Normal are twin cities separated by a street aptly called Division Street. They are located in McLean County with Bloomington being the county seat. The twin cities are located 130 miles south of Chicago, Illinois, and 180 miles north of St. Louis, Missouri. Route 66 passes through the twin cities as it travels from Chicago to Santa Monica, California.

Normal was originally called North Bloomington when it was founded by Joseph Parkinson in 1854. The first addition to North Bloomington was developed by Jesse W. Fell in 1857. Fell was a friend of Abraham Lincoln and a founder of *The Daily Pantagraph*, the local newspaper.

Later in 1865 the name was changed to Normal presumably because a normal school had been built in Normal. Fell had led the effort to get the first normal school in Illinois to be located in Bloomington, although the school ended up being built in Normal. Normal schools were two-year teacher training schools. That school continued to grow, becoming known as Illinois State Normal University (ISNU), and later was renamed Illinois State University (ISU) in 1964. Normal is most known for ISU.

Linden Street was originally called Chicago Street and formed the eastern boundary of the original town. Just one block west of Linden was the Illinois Central railroad tracks. (That track is now a nature/bicycle path called Constitution Trail.) One more block west was Broadway Avenue, and the next block west was Fell Avenue. Fell Avenue was named after Jesse W. Fell. Fell had his home constructed on Fell Avenue.

For 100 years Normal was a dry town, meaning no intoxicating drinks could be sold within town limits.

Bloomington is most known for State Farm Insurance since it was founded in Bloomington in 1922 and its home office is located here. State Farm's founder, George J. Mecherle, grew up in Merna, Illinois, just nine miles east of Bloomington. Mecherle founded State Farm when he was 45 years old and grew the company at a rapid pace. (I remember when the available office space in Bloomington had been filled completely by State Farm. They would build a new building and then see it rapidly filled to capacity. Then another building would be constructed. And so it went. It was very difficult for a State Farm employee to have lunch or dinner anywhere in town and talk about confidential business matters since there was always a high probability that one or more other State Farm employees would be close by and hear every word.)

We had two universities in Bloomington-Normal. Bloomington had Illinois Wesleyan University (IWU), a private university, and Normal had ISNU, a public university. The two campuses were situated at opposite ends of Franklin Avenue. *Ripley's Believe It or Not!* once published: "Franklin Avenue in Bloomington, Illinois is the only street in the United States to have a university at either end."

I had a personal accomplishment related to Franklin Avenue. This would have been around 1950. I rode my bicycle from the ISNU end of Franklin Avenue all the way to the IWU end with my hands off the handlebars! This was on a slightly uphill ride. No one was watching so I guess I didn't make it into Ripley's or Guinness World Records.

Sometime shortly after 1988, BroMenn Hospital in Normal started an ambitious expansion program that required blocking off Franklin Avenue at West Virginia Avenue on its north side to allow them to expand westward. To get to the southern blocked-off area of Franklin Avenue, one had to travel west one block to South University Street, turn left and go to Apple Street, turn left and go one block and turn right on Franklin. Then one could travel south to reach IWU. Thus, there was no longer a direct route between ISNU and IWU on Franklin Avenue.

However, University Street did extend north to ISNU, and it also traveled down directly to touch IWU. Using University Street to connect ISNU and IWU, one is always in Normal. In the Ripley statement, Franklin Avenue was in Bloomington. That was never strictly true since Franklin was mostly in Normal. But, from that point on, people around the area were saying that University Street in Normal was the only Street in the United States with a university at either end.

There was a bridge over the Illinois Central train tracks that every person living in Bloomington-Normal has been over. Even visitors to Bloomington-Normal are told about the bridge, so they won't miss the opportunity to drive over it. They are also cautioned not to drive very fast. The bridge is called the Camelback Bridge. It was named to the National Register of Historic Places in 1997. The wooden bridge had what is called a Kingpost superstructure and Phoenix columns. At one time it became damaged by the old locomotive smokestacks that would burn the wood as the train passed under the bridge.

Most folks in Bloomington-Normal weren't much aware of the structural problems or the historical significance of the Camelback Bridge. They just liked to drive their cars over it and feel the rumbling of the wood planks under their tires.

As you approached the bridge, you couldn't see over it. You just left the regular street surface and went up on the wood planks at a gradual slant, and then your car would be on the flat top wood surface, and suddenly be horizontal for several car lengths. After that, the car would dip down as it left the flatness and continue down onto the other side, where the rumbling continued for another car length or so, and the regular street surface reappeared. If you happened to be unaware of how the bridge behaved and had too much speed, it could become a thrill ride with an unpredictable outcome.

In May 1979, according to an account in *The Daily Pantagraph*, six ISU students found this out first hand. After celebrating the upcoming end of the school year in their apartment and at a local tavern, they started home after 2:00 a.m. and hit the bridge at between 65 and 71 mph, lost control, and literally flew off the bridge 82 feet in the air before they struck the street and slid an additional 367 feet into a wall before coming to rest. Two people died including the driver, who was found to have an elevated blood alcohol level of 0.148. (One of the few letters I received from my dad, dated May 7, 1979, mentioned this same incident.)

The Camelback Bridge still exists today, and I ride over it at least once every time I'm home—at low speed. The bridge has been substantially improved from an engineering standpoint, but it still has the same features that placed it on the National Register, although they are now mostly cosmetic.

3. My Family

When I was a kid growing up in Normal, time always moved slowly. Days dragged by. School dragged by. My social life dragged as well.

I remember growing up with no grandparents around. My mother, Margaret, born in 1908, had lost both of her parents before she was 23 years old. Margaret was the oldest of six children. She assumed the major role of mother for her siblings after her mother's death in 1931.

Margaret came from a large Irish Catholic family, most of whom lived in Bloomington. Margaret's mother was Johanna Watson, who was the fifth of 10 children. Johanna was born in 1881 and died in 1931. Margaret's father was Paul Gleason, born in 1882 and died in 1930. Paul was a railroad engineer from Pennsylvania who moved to Aurora, Illinois, and then to Bloomington, where he worked in the Chicago & Alton (C&A) Shops. Johanna's mother was Catherine Sheahan (1853-1932), and her father was Luke Watson, Sr. (1842-1919). (Early in my writing career, I used Luke Watson as a pseudonym.)

I knew very little about Dad's family. I knew his surname was Kern and he had grown up in Bedford, Indiana. I knew his mother, Minnie, had been born in Kentucky and moved to Bedford early on. I surmised that I had Irish roots from my mom and, most likely, Germanic roots from my grandfather Kern but I didn't know Minnie's background. I'm sure that as a kid, I didn't care much about where I came from. My need for knowledge of my heritage would wait for me to mature and come to understand that I had secrets that I needed to uncover first.

Mom and Dad were married in Danvers, Illinois, in September 1934. Both of them were 26 years old. They lived on East Beecher Street in Bloomington then moved to Normal after my sister and I were born.

Mom would get an occasional handwritten letter from Williams, Indiana, from my grandmother, Minnie Lee Kern, but we never visited her and she never visited us. I don't even remember reading any of these letters, although I know that Mom did read some passages to my sister, Kay (born in 1939), my brother, Ronald (born in 1948), and me. Kay was 23 months younger than me, while Ronald was 10-1/2 years younger than me. Depending on my age, I knew Ronald as Ronnie, then Ron.

In Mom's high school yearbook, *Trinitas* (1926), the description next to her picture reads: "A knowledge seeker and a diligent worker." She liked reading books and was a skilled stenographer/typist working at the Relief Office in Bloomington when she met Dad. She used to tell my sister and me, "I had a book under my arm, and he had a radio under his." She kept a steno pad at home and often wrote notes or pages in shorthand.

I heard nothing about my grandfather, Earl Kern, except that he was a farmer. Dad told us only the good parts about his parents, but we always suspected that there was an undercurrent of distrust by my father against Earl and vice versa. Dad was the oldest child in his family of seven Kern children. I had heard him talk about some of his siblings from time to time, but they were unknown to me personally.

Dad worked as a foreman at Williams Oil-O-Matic in Bloomington. (In 1925 Walter W. Williams built the first successful oil burner that used a control mechanism to make the oil burner automatic. The Williams Oil-O-Matic factory manufactured these heaters and shipped them all over the world. In June 1945 Williams merged with vacuum cleaner maker Eureka to become Eureka-Williams. Today the company is known as Electrolux.)

I was told that Dad had made it only to the fifth grade in Bedford, Indiana, when he dropped out of school. Mom made it all the way through school and graduated from Saint Mary's Catholic High

School in Bloomington. Their three kids would be graduating from high school, too. Both Kay and I would not stop there.

We lived in a corner house on South Linden Street. It was a two-story house built in the late 1890s. It was heated by a coal-fired furnace in the basement. The water heater was also in the basement, but it was not automatic. You had to walk down the stairs to the basement and manually light the heater to get it going. Then you had to wait for the water to heat before you could take a bath or use hot water anywhere.

A monumental improvement came when Dad installed a "Step-Saver" button in the bathroom. When you first got up, you pressed the button, a red light came on, and the downstairs water heater fired up automatically. It was like magic! But, you still had to wait for the water to heat.

When visitors stepped onto the small covered front porch from Linden Street and entered the front door, they saw a long hallway with a closed door at the end. In the middle of the hallway on the right side was a white wooden telephone stand recessed into the wall. It was previously used as a telephone stand for an upstairs apartment, but the telephone had been removed. To the left of the front door was the bathroom (the only one in the house), and to the right of the front door was my bedroom. The stairs, along the left side of the hallway, had a banister that Kay, Ron, and I slid down every chance we got for fun.

Our bathroom was next to a second bedroom.

When I was very young, tenants renting the upstairs apartment from us had their own kitchen and two other rooms that could be either two bedrooms or one bedroom and a living room. They also shared the bathroom at the foot of the stairs.

I don't remember the tenants at all. (I know that they existed because I found them in the 1940 Federal Census, living in our house.) I'm sure that with two families using one bathroom, life must have been hectic at times. My Aunt Nellie, Mom's sister, also lived with us until she got married in 1941. I have no idea where she slept unless Kay and I were in the same bedroom. I would have been no older than three, while Kay was a one-year-old.

The door at the end of the hallway led to the living room. If you opened it, turned right, and walked a few steps, you would see the second door to my bedroom. If you turned left from the hallway, you would enter the dining room. The dining room had a high ceiling and a chandelier hanging in the center over the dining room table, which seated eight people. Mom used this table for holiday dinners. Kay, Ron, and I used it for cards and board games like Monopoly. We also spread out our books and papers on it to do homework and school projects.

Off the dining room to the left was the second bedroom, which faced the street. (It also adjoined the bathroom.) Off the dining room to the right was the kitchen.

The basement had two points of entry. One was from the dining room. If you turned left after entering the dining room from the living room, you saw a door. You entered the basement from that door. An overhead light barely lit the steep wooden steps that led down to a concrete floor. The other entrance was from the outside. The south side of the house had a passageway covered by two wooden doors that you pulled up, one by one, and laid to the side. You then descended steps to a regular door that led into the basement.

In the early days, we had a coal-fired furnace in the basement and an associated coal bin under the living room. Coal was delivered by truck and dumped down a chute from the back of the truck into the coal bin. The coal made quite a racket sliding down the chute! I remember sitting on the sofa right over the coal bin just listening while the coal was delivered.

Dad fired the coal furnace using a heavy shovel to scoop up a load of coal from the coal bin, carry it maybe 20 feet to the front of the furnace, and toss it through the open furnace door. That process was repeated until Dad felt that the fire was of sufficient size to maintain itself for a while. As the coal burned, the ashes had to be removed. A sifting mechanism under the fire pit allowed ashes to drop, and Dad removed them through another door under the fire pit. The ashes were used outside to pour on the sidewalk and driveway. (In those days there was no salt to buy for that purpose.)

I'm not sure how the fire was started in the first place, but I think Dad just burned whatever paper we happened to have on hand until the coal caught fire. (I do remember burning some letters in there. That will be covered later.) A few years later Dad converted to gas heat and the coal bin became only an empty, damp, dark place in the basement.

We had a large walk-in closet, located immediately to the right when you entered the dining room from the living room. The closet was entered through a door. A window in the closet provided extra light. The closet was next to a white wooden telephone stand recessed into the dining room wall. (This stand was exactly like the one in the hallway, described earlier.) When I was on the phone, I would take the telephone into the closet extending the extra-long telephone cord, sit on the floor, and close the door for privacy.

When Mom was on the phone, sometimes Kay, Ron, and I were too boisterous and noisy for her to listen. She always kept a large wooden hairbrush with black bristles next to the phone. She would just raise it in the air and stare at us to keep us in line. Just the threat to use the hairbrush was enough to quiet us down.

In the kitchen, we had a natural-gas stove with a high oven to one side that was old-fashioned. (I believe it was replaced once with a lower unit with a bottom oven while I lived in the house.) Our wooden kitchen table, kept covered with easy-care oilcloth, was directly in the center of the kitchen. The refrigerator was to the left as you entered the kitchen from the dining room. Cabinets lined the north wall. Two doors led to the outside from the kitchen. The door to the left of the stove led to a south porch with brick steps but was never used for anything except a direct exit to the side yard.

The other door (we called it the "back door") was next to the kitchen sink. This door was rarely locked for some reason. It led to a covered, screened-in porch. There was no window over the sink, only a wall. Mom always wished for a window there, but it was never made a reality for her.

In the winter, the heat came into most rooms through large floor grates I called "registers." I would always sit on these registers every morning to get warm. I would come out of my bedroom in the morning and immediately sit on the register in the living room. There was a small register just as you entered the dining room from the living room and another large register as you turned right into the kitchen. I would visit all three of these registers each day on my way to breakfast.

We had an old weather-beaten garage that was separated from the house. We could go out through the kitchen, walk across the back porch, and down several brick steps to a pathway of individual bricks set a few feet apart and reach the garage in maybe 10 steps. Dad had strung a heavy-duty electrical cord from the kitchen wall outlet, through a hole in the outside wall, across the top of the porch, and tightly rigged to the garage. It was then fed through the garage wall and connected inside to light bulb sockets and outlets.

The garage had a tightly packed dirt floor and two wide doors that swung open to receive a car. The doors connected to a large wooden rail in the center. The rail stretched completely across the width of the garage. It looked like a leftover from the days when a horse and buggy might have been stored there instead of a car.

A workbench occupied most of the length of the garage with tools placed here and there. Dad was a mechanic and once had owned his own garage in Indiana. He had tools to work on his car. If he needed a tool he didn't have, he could make it. He would come out to the unheated garage in the winter and work on his Chrysler. The cold never seemed to bother him.

In front of where a car might have been parked was a wall. In that wall was an entryway to an area just big enough to house the various motors and machines that Dad used. (He had built most of them.) Another wider outside door allowed entry to, and exit from, this storage space. He had built both a self-propelled tractor and a self-propelled lawn mower. He had a single motor that he would remove from one of these machines and install on the other, depending on which machine he wanted to use. In the spring and fall, he would use the tractor to prepare his extensive gardens that covered nearly two of his three lots. The garden was massive. You could tell that he was used to farming as he had spent the first 17 years of his life living and working on his dad's farm in Williams, Indiana.

A portion of the garden produced food items that Mom used daily. She canned the rest of the food items and stored them on shelves in the basement for future use. Thus, we had a ready supply of peaches, jellies, beans, tomatoes, pears, peas, applesauce, etc.

The two lots and the corner lot upon which the house sat had been part of the original town of Normal as it was laid out in 1854. The lots were bought and sold many times, and owners tried to keep all three lots together. Dad was no exception. He had many opportunities to sell the other two lots but never did. He liked having all that space around his house even though there was a continual passage of kids cutting through the property to save a few steps on their way to school. When Dad tended the garden, there was no easy way to cut through. When he finally gave up gardening and let the grass grow, the foot traffic was constant and annoying.

Dad also had a small machine shop in the basement that included a drill press and a small lathe. He could make or repair almost any part down there. I was continually amazed at his innate mechanical and electrical ability. He could fix anything, it seemed. Women in the neighborhood often brought their broken household items (irons, toasters, fans, etc.) to "Walt," and he always got them humming again.

After the upstairs tenants had left for good, Dad converted the upstairs living room into a radio shop and used the bedroom for Mom and him. By that time Kay had the bedroom next to the bathroom, and Ron and I shared the other bedroom. As I've said, we all shared that one Jack and Jill bathroom.

Dad developed a small business called the Kern Radio Service. He repaired radios. Mom took care of his business accounts. That brought in more money to supplement his work at Williams Oil-O-Matic. I used to go with him sometimes on his radio repair calls. I would sit in his 1933 Chrysler and wait for him.

The radio shop had a junk closet and lots of handbuilt floor-to-ceiling shelves packed with radio vacuum tubes and other necessary radio spare parts. One wall had a giant electrical board mounted on it. Underneath the board was a workbench. The board had seemingly hundreds of red, green, and black terminals, outlets, testing equipment, a vice, soldering irons and mountings, electrical meters and gauges, etc. It was a great place to experiment and learn about radios, but I was strongly encouraged to stay away unless Dad was there supervising me.

There was a leftover davenport (couch or sofa) in one corner of the radio shop and a couple of windows where you could look out on Linden Street and watch the cars flying by at 30 mph (the standard speed on most streets in Normal and Bloomington). It was in this radio shop that I first saw black-and-white TV on a three-by-five-inch video screen when hardly anyone in town even had a TV set. Dad had experimented with TV, but he continued with what he knew—radio—and refused to get involved fixing television sets. Technology was then advancing too rapidly for him to keep up.

Dad once mentioned that he built a radio with a loudspeaker and used to place it on a hill in Indiana and broadcast down into the valley. He called himself one of the first radio disc jockeys.

He also said he developed a vibrator for a car radio. This is not the same vibrator that you may be thinking of. The vibrator converted 6-volt DC car battery power into 50-volt to 250-volt DC to power a radio containing large vacuum tubes. (There were no transistors to replace tubes at that time. Transistors were invented in 1948 by Bell Labs, and it took many more years to perfect them and manufacture them for general use.) Dad's one-off vibrator was ahead of its time. Dad told me that when he heard that a vibrator had been used commercially in a car radio, he knew that even though he had been one of the first to perfect one, he would never receive any credit for it. (One successful car radio that was widely sold later was called a Motor Victrola or Motor-ola. It used a vibrator. The success of the Motor-ola radio resulted in the formation of the Motorola Company.)

Dad said that when he had traveled West as a young man, he often ended up in jobs where he wound coils for electric motors. He got very good at it and once convinced his boss that the coils could be wound more efficiently. The boss wanted a demonstration. Dad complied by showing the boss how to do it himself. Dad became the star employee for that. But then he moved on. He always got homesick and had to return to Indiana.

There was no air-conditioning in those days. We had screens in the windows, and we kept the windows open. Several large fans circulated the air. There was always a droning sound of rushing air in the summertime. In the winter, Dad installed storm windows.

The rooms in our house had plaster walls covered with wallpaper installed by Mr. Wiese, who was the father of several of my neighborhood playmates.

4. The War Years

I was almost four years old when Japan bombed Pearl Harbor on December 7, 1941. I knew next to nothing about the actual war. However, I do remember a few notable things that occurred during the war years.

Dad continued to work for Williams Oil-O-Matic, but the factory was now manufacturing to support the war effort. He exercised his considerable mechanical abilities at Williams since he had several physical problems including eyesight that precluded him from serving in the armed forces. He was 33 years old in 1941.

Since there was so much secrecy during the war, I did not know what Dad's contribution to the war effort was. I found out later as an adult. Dad was in a group of key men at Williams that took on government requests for automated features to help defeat Nazi Germany. One such request was to produce a hydraulically controlled automatic antiaircraft firing mechanism. Unfortunately, the plans for the device were on board a ship from England that had been sunk. Dad and other key men had to disassemble a working model of the device, figure out how it worked, and then create ways to manufacture all the parts and assemble them on a mass scale. They completed the project with time to spare and under budget.

I have faint recollections of life in Normal during the war. I remember rationing. Sale of items such as shoes, gasoline, coffee, and sugar was tightly controlled with coupons and Office of Price Administration (OPA) stamps, coins and chits for rationing. OPA coins (commonly called OPAs or tokens) were used for change for food. OPAs were used by retailers to give change back for food bought with ration stamps. Blue tokens were used for processed foods, and red tokens were used for meats and fats. OPAs were first issued in 1944 and stopped being issued in 1945.

My mother would collect grease from cooking and place it in large cans to be set outside to cool. At the time, I was unaware where the grease went. (I now read that these cans of grease were returned to the grocery store or butcher where they would pass the grease on to the war effort and then return the can to the homeowner. Even the empty cans were returned so they could be recycled.) I remember war bonds being purchased. (Williams Oil-O-Matic deducted ten percent from wages to purchase war bonds for each employee.)

For some reason, I recall my Uncle Hardy being at our house and he was talking on the telephone to the draft board. It was the telephone that we had in the dining room. I was in the bedroom next to the bathroom, and I could see him hunched over the recessed wooden phone stand, described earlier. Uncle Hardy's real name was Lawrence Hardesty, but for some reason, everyone called him "Hardy." Hardy was married to my mom's sister, Nellie. I know they were married just a few months before Pearl Harbor was bombed. I don't know why he was calling—or maybe they were calling him—but I do know that he did not have to serve. He was about 24 years old at the time.

5. Normal Central School Years

In 1944 I entered grade school at Normal Central School at the age of six years and eight months. Mom did not send me to kindergarten. Almost every other kid in my class had been to kindergarten. (Kay told me when I was writing this memoir, "Mom just couldn't bear to let us go to school since there was no requirement for kindergarten.") In spite of this late start to learning, I did well in school and made friends although I was on the shy side (and still am). Kay, although almost two years younger than me, was only one year behind me in school—undoubtedly because my birthday was in January 1938 and Kay's was in December 1939. They must have accepted a student into first grade if they became six years old in that year.

I know that today, families celebrate the first day of school whether it's kindergarten or first grade and are a little sad that the child is leaving on a school bus. They also dread the time that their child leaves for college. The sadness then is more tearful. I don't remember much about the first day I went to Normal Central School. I believe that Mom walked over there with me on a trial run so I would know where to go and what route to take. The school provided safety patrols at all the corners near the school. These were students, not adults. I'm not sure I knew about the safety patrols. I probably found out when I ventured out to go to my first day of school, alone.

I remember when my third-grade teacher popped me on the back of my head with a pencil and told me to stop talking. I told her that I had not said a word. She never apologized. I remember my sixth-grade teacher who took us on a class trip to Springfield to visit Illinois Governor Adlai Stevenson. He was her second cousin. He wasn't in the office that day, but we all got a chance to sit in his chair behind his desk. I also remember gym class where I found out that I was one of the fastest runners at completing a mile run.

Normal Central School was purchased by Illinois State University (ISU) and demolished in 1974 to erect student residence halls. Normal Central School had been in existence from 1912 to 1974.

I remember having a good time roaming the neighborhood in Normal. We only lived four blocks from the center of town. There were two railroads that crossed in Normal. One, the Illinois Central, passed a block west of my house and the other, the Chicago and Alton, crossed Linden Street four blocks north of my house. Both railroads first arrived in Normal in 1853.

All my neighborhood friends before I went to high school lived close by. To me, there were two major families: Wiese and Shutt. Each family had many children. I was never quite sure how many there were in each family since the ages spilled over many years. There were always some kids that had left home and might be married. There were little kids that were too young for me, and then there were those that might fall a few years younger or a few years older than me. The result was that there was a group of kids that numbered maybe 15 to 20 that congregated, mainly at the Wiese house either in the street, on the front porch, the back driveway where the basketball hoop was, or inside the house.

I usually walked over or rode my bike. The group would play until it got dark and then slowly disband as kids were called home or went home on their own. I was usually too far away from home for me to hear anyone yelling for me so I just went home when I knew my parents would expect me. I can't remember ever doing anything that harmed another person. My sister Kay was in that group also. I spent most of my time with Merle, and Kay played most with his sister, Betty. They were both from the Wiese family.

My neighborhood friends and I also walked to school together. We all went to Normal Central School that was eight blocks away. This school covered kindergarten to eighth grade. We walked almost all the time except sometimes in the winter, one of the older kids might pick us up in their car as we walked along.

What did we do? We rode bicycles, played baseball, basketball, catch, croquet, kick the can, and hide and go seek. We talked and told stories. We ate a lot of popcorn. No one drank, smoked or took drugs. The mothers and fathers always had control, and we respected their wishes. We all had strict parents. Mary Ann Shutt, who was in my grade, convinced me to join her church. I had not gone to any church before. Mom was a Catholic, but Dad had no religion that I could see. Mom didn't make any attempt to take us to the Catholic church, so when Mary Ann pressed me to go to her church, Mom agreed, and I became a Presbyterian for most of my grade school years. Then I dropped out for most of high school.

I used to ride my bicycle over to visit my neighborhood friends. Once, I was acting up on the bike going back and forth on the block where the Wiese family lived. (I may have even put a piece of cardboard to a spoke using a clothes pin to make the bike sound like a motorcycle. Riding real motorcycles would take more than 40 years to become a reality for me.) The edge of the road was replete with shallow potholes, some with gravel. I was passing through these potholes when suddenly I lost my balance and fell striking my arm on the ground. I looked down and saw a lot of blood and a wound about two inches from my elbow on my forearm. Kids rushed over to me but were ill equipped to do anything for me, so I got back on the bike and rode the two blocks to my house. Mom cleaned the wound, put Mercurochrome on it, and covered it with a bandage. We didn't go to the hospital or call a doctor. It was the worst injury I had as a child. When it healed after a month or two, a blemish remained that was visible for years, maybe as long as 30 years. (As I look at it now in 2016, I see nothing at all, as if the injury never even happened.)

My brother, Ron, was born in 1948 when I was 10 years old. When Ron was walking and playing in the neighborhood, he was worrisome to me. I had seen him wander off and play on the railroad tracks. I even saw him walking on the rails. I was worried for his safety. There were no crossing gates, but there were flashing red lights when a train was approaching. You were never sure how fast a given train was going. Sometimes there would be switching going on or other low-speed activity. Other times the train was just passing through at high speed. When I got out of school, I always hurried home by walking along the tracks. Sometimes I would also walk on the rails seeing how far I could balance on a rail before I lost my balance and fell off. I was always careful, but I feared that Ron would get hit by a train. Fortunately, that never happened, but I probably lost a tiny bit of my lifespan worrying that it would.

Another time when Ron was six or seven years old, we found out that he had walked south on Linden Street a few blocks past our house, turned left, and walked a few more blocks to reach a chicken farm. We don't know why, but Ron proceeded to enter several chicken coops and throw every egg he could find in all directions. He never had a clear rationale for why he thought this was a good playtime activity. I'm pretty sure Dad ended up paying for the damage, but maybe not.

I also recall a few disturbing incidents.

One occurred when I was walking home from grade school by myself. I was on Broadway Avenue about a block away from where I would turn left on the street that would lead to my house. I was only three blocks from home. I became concerned when I noticed an enormous kid (or man) approaching me on the sidewalk. When we were next to each other, he suddenly, without warning, reached down, grabbed me by my feet, and upended me—holding me vertically with my head about six inches from the brick sidewalk. I thought he was going to kill me! Then, just as suddenly, he flipped me onto the grass and went on his way, not uttering a single word. I was in tranquil, quiet, and peaceful Normal, Illinois, in the late forties. Nothing like this had ever happened to me before. After that, I was terrified to take that same route home from school. I never wanted to run into him again.

The second incident occurred when I had a pup tent set up in my side yard about five feet in from the sidewalk on Linden Street close to the southern border of our property. I was in the tent when a paperboy came up the sidewalk walking north and saw me. He dropped his paper bag, jumped into the tent with me, and started putting his hands all over me. This was a new, different, and unwanted experience for me. I did not know what was going on, but I knew it was wrong. I got out of the tent as fast as I could and told him to leave me alone! He left without explanation. It was my first (and only) unwelcome sexual experience. I never saw him again. I don't know if I told anyone about this. I just knew it was wrong, even though no one had ever warned me that there were people like this in the world. I distinctly remember his name to this day, but I won't use it here. I hope he eventually got caught and got punished.

The last incident occurred when I saw a "dirty" book and heard about prostitutes from a kid in school. I think it was on a playground somewhere. I saw a bunch of boys huddled together, talking and laughing about something. I went over to see what was going on. The kid showed me a small book, maybe the size of a recipe card. It was black and white with ragged edges on the pages. It had pictures of obese women in bed with nasty things going on. He also told me that these women were prostitutes or whores. Then to my great surprise, he said that Bloomington had a street where there were many prostitutes living in the houses. You could drive down the street and see the prostitutes looking out the windows motioning for you to stop and visit them. I thought that this was ridiculous. I didn't believe him. That couldn't be happening in Bloomington. Unfortunately, it was all true. I was slowly learning about the world. That street is still there, but it has a new name; however, the houses and the prostitutes are gone.

While in grade school, all students were subjected to a periodic scalp examination in the nurse's office to detect ringworm (dermatophytosis). In all my years of grade school, I had only seen two boys with ringworm. Unfortunately, I was one of them. According to the modern definition of ringworm, it is a fungal infection of the skin. "Ringworm" is a misnomer. The infection isn't caused by a worm; it's caused by a fungus. Often the treatment will take care of the infection in a month or less; however, I was living in the forties. I was required to use some smelly substance on my scalp daily and then cover the top of my head with a homemade hairnet-like cap stretched tightly over my hair. The cap was made out of the end of an old silk stocking from Mom. I remember having a pile of these stockings that had come from Mom and her relatives. Having to wear this symbol of disease was about as embarrassing to me as being forced to come to class naked! If I was shy before, I was now painfully diffident. I had to wear the cap for many months—maybe even longer than a year—until I got a medical release. By that time, I had almost totally withdrawn into myself. I don't remember when this was, perhaps in the fourth or fifth grade. I don't even want to remember.

6. Mom

Sometime after my brother Ron was born in 1948, I became aware that my mother was not her usual self. She did strange things around the house and talked in an unusual manner.

I was a kid about 10 years old, and I didn't process family matters that well. Finally, one day my mother was no longer there. Dad said he had to take her to Peoria State Hospital in Peoria, Illinois, to get treatment. He would drive over there every so often, and sometimes I would go, too.

Dad was driving his 1933 4-door Chrysler sedan. It had a manual transmission with a long gearshift lever rising out of the center of the floor. (Automatic transmissions were introduced in 1940 in the Oldsmobile as a Hydra-Matic; but because of the war and the cessation of automobile production, automatics only started to catch on in the late forties.) The rear seat side and rear windows had canvas shades with tassel-like cords that could be pulled down to completely cover the window either for privacy or shade. The upholstery was a fuzzy brown that some people called mouse hair. I wasn't allowed to go inside the hospital so I just waited in the car. Things were safer in those days.

Kay and I were left on our own while Dad was working. I don't know exactly how old we were when Mom was in Peoria State Hospital. On weekdays we would lock up the house before school and let ourselves in after school. Then there was perhaps a one- to two-hour window before Dad came home from work. I don't know if there was an equivalent to Child Protective Services at that time. If there was, then I guess we slipped through the cracks. At any rate, I believe that we were mature enough to take care of ourselves with no problems occurring and were learning how to be independent at an earlier age than most kids. We lived only eight blocks from Normal Central School and sometimes would walk home for lunch. Dad had made lunch for us, and we just took it out of the refrigerator.

I particularly remember times when Dad would make chocolate pudding with layers of graham crackers. That was a treat.

The biggest problem Dad had at this time was taking care of baby Ron. Dad still worked at Williams Oil-O-Matic in Bloomington (as he would continue to do for his remaining work life) and was away from the house from 6:30 a.m. to 4:30 p.m. We had no outside help, but Dad found out that there was a place in Normal called The Baby Fold that would take in Ron for the time that Mom was in the hospital. (The Baby Fold was founded in 1902 by Nancy Mason, who gave her home to further the work of the Methodist Episcopal Church. She opened her home to be used by active and retired Methodist Deaconesses who operated Deaconess Hospital. It evolved through the years, offering an array of services to young children.) Thus, Kay and I took regular trips with Dad to Peoria to see Mom and to The Baby Fold in Normal to see our baby brother. I don't remember how long this situation lasted but certainly no more than a few months. Then Mom and her three kids were back together in our house, at least for a while.

As I got older, I found out that Peoria State Hospital was a psychiatric hospital in Bartonville, Illinois (near Peoria). I don't know what caused Mom's mental state to deteriorate; but as I look back, she might have been in postpartum depression. I know she did not drive and depended on Dad to drive her wherever she needed to go. We never seemed to have much money, and that worried her. (Mom saved quarters in an Alka-Seltzer bottle so we could have occasional treats, such as an ice cream cone from Tastee-Freez.)

I was told that Mom had received electroshock treatments in Peoria State Hospital. These treatments were fairly new then, and no one knew why they worked. Some thought they had the effect of resetting the brain to a normal state. However, there was concern that they were painful to undergo and possibly dangerous. Mom never talked much about her treatments. She just seemed normal to me when she came home, almost as if she had just returned from a restful vacation on a tropical island. These treatments are now called electroconvulsive therapy (ECT) and seem to be performed with more controls than were present in the 1940s when Mom underwent them. Here is a definition of ECT from the Mayo Clinic website (www.mayoclinic.org):

> "Electroconvulsive therapy (ECT) is a procedure, done under general anesthesia, in which small electric currents are passed through the brain, intentionally triggering a brief seizure. ECT seems to cause changes in brain chemistry that can quickly reverse symptoms of certain mental illnesses. It often works when other treatments are unsuccessful."

I remember a lot of hushed arguments between my parents. Once when Mom and Dad were upstairs near the door to the radio shop, I heard them arguing. Then I saw Mom at the head of the stairs, with Dad behind her. The argument got louder. I was afraid that Mom might get thrown down the staircase, but that never happened. Lack of money seemed to be the cause of most of their disagreements. (Ron recently told me that he recalled seeing Mom crying on the bottom step of the staircase after an argument with Dad.)

Periodically, Mom would slip back into a depression, or get severely agitated, and Dad would have to take her back to Peoria for an extended stay.

I recall one night when Dad had to call the police because Mom was out of control. A police car pulled up in front of our house and parked on Linden Street with its lights flashing. Two police officers walked up the short brick sidewalk, ascended the four steps to the covered porch, and rang the doorbell. Dad hurried to the front door and let the police officers into the foyer (we always called it the "hallway"). I couldn't understand what was going on. Mom and Dad were having a heated discussion, mostly about how Mom was acting, when Mom screamed, "He never has anything in the house. There isn't even any soap."

One officer, seeing that I was upset, took me aside and said, "Walter, do you know where Mommy keeps the soap?" (I was probably five or six years old.)

Trying to be helpful, I replied, "It's out in the kitchen under the sink."

The officer, I'm sure, was just trying to get me away from the grown-up situation that was going on when he said, "Let's go see if we can find the soap. You lead the way." I remember running out to the kitchen and bending down to open the two doors in the cabinet under the kitchen sink. I pulled out a pack of soap bars and handed it to the officer. He thanked me and said, "Good boy. It looks like you have soap. You can put it back now." Then he tried to talk to me some more while the other officer tried to resolve the situation.

I'm not sure what happened next. I remember being led outside into the darkness along with my sister, and walking to our next-door neighbor's house. They were the Baylor family. (I would find out many years later that Mrs. Baylor was the sister of my future wife's brother-in-law.) We stayed with the Baylor family for a few days while Dad sorted out all the details to get Mom admitted to Peoria State Hospital.

I remember one more time when I was in junior high. I came home from school and found Mom distraught and rambling incoherently in the dining room. This was a frightening incident for me. I felt powerless to help my mother who was in obvious distress. It was a sight I have never been able to get out of my mind. When Dad came home from work, he spoke with Mom for a while trying to assess the situation. In a day or two, Mom was readmitted to Peoria State Hospital.

While Mom was in Peoria this time, I had an opportunity to go with Uncle Hardy, Aunt Nellie, and their children (my cousins) for a day at Lake Bloomington, about 20 miles from our house. Hardy was very talkative and boisterous. You could hear him a long way off. Dad wasn't interested in going to the Lake. I think I was the only

Kern kid that went. (Lake Bloomington was the water supply for Bloomington. It was also a recreational area for swimming, boating, and fishing. The Lake was surrounded by homes that were owned by companies and individuals.)

I'm not sure why I went on this excursion. I was not a swimmer. I didn't boat. I didn't fish. I guess I was there just to get away from Normal for a day and get some sun. It was hot, and I had swim trunks on. I remember my cousins getting in the water and wading out a bit. I thought I would try that, too, so I followed them. Hardy and Aunt Nellie stayed sitting on the sand. Suddenly I felt the ground go out from under me. Down I went!

There must have been a drop-off, and it got me. I went straight down and I was flailing around trying to get back up to the surface. I could see a circular well-lit section of the water's surface above me. It was the sun beaming down a message that I was in trouble, and something had better happen quickly if I were ever to see the sun again. Then everything went dark.

I don't know how much time passed. Then I was aware that I was back on the beach, wrapped in a blanket. I asked what had happened. Apparently, my uncle had tried to rescue me but couldn't and had yelled for help across the lake. He did have a loud voice, and someone on the other side heard him and immediately got in his car and raced to where I was. The stranger jumped in, pulled me out, and performed artificial respiration on me until I came around. He then left, almost immediately, and we never saw him again. I'm sure he was an angel dispatched to save me. I asked how I got rescued and who did it. All my uncle could say was, "Someone from across the lake came over and pulled you out. I think he said he was an ISNU student."

That's all I ever heard. I remember asking Uncle Hardy, "Why did he leave? I wanted to thank him for saving me." I meant every word.

Dad said that Mom should never hear about this near-tragic incident. He didn't want to take a chance that it might push her over the edge into another stay in Peoria. So I never mentioned it to Mom, and neither did anyone else in my family. We were beginning to learn how to keep family secrets.

I want to emphasize that my family life growing up was very harmonious and beneficial for my siblings and me. We had a loving environment. Mom was always our advocate with Dad when we needed help convincing him of the desirability of some activity about which Dad had concerns.

Mom had professional pictures taken of Kay and me when we were young. One picture, probably done by Camera Craft in Normal, showed us seated on a bench. Kay held a doll while I had a rifle over my shoulder. Mom purchased two-cent postcards from Camera Craft with the picture on the back. Kay found one of the postcards that Mom had sent to a relative. Mom had written on the card, "A letter will be on its way shortly, but I had to send my darlings (when they're sleeping) picture on ahead. Something to be proud of don't you think?" It was postmarked August 6, 1945. The date seemed strangely familiar. It was the same day that the first atomic bomb was dropped on Hiroshima, Japan, during the final stage of World War II.

7. Normal Remembrances

The Normal Tomato Festival was a town event that started in 1948 and ended in 1952. We had at least three tomato processors in Bloomington-Normal. One was in Normal close to where I lived. In September there were tomatoes all over town to be picked. There were ads in *The Daily Pantagraph* for tomato pickers.

A Normal real estate company decided that it would be a good idea to have a town festival built around tomatoes. It would attract visitors and be good for local business. It would also get people out of their houses to walk all over town. Tomato juice stands were set up on every corner, offering free tomato juice. I used to walk to grade school and passed right through the center of town. Every time I walked by one of those stands, I was handed a paper cup of tomato juice. I'm sure I had a red mustache when I got to school.

Besides the free tomato juice, there were other events and displays that dealt with tomatoes. There was a cooking school in the Normal Theatre, for example, that I'm sure must have required tomatoes as an ingredient in recipes.

In 1951 the Normal Tomato Festival went into the red (pun intended) when someone caught on to the fact that a Bingo game was being allowed out in the open. That was gambling! The State of Illinois shut the game down, and the Festival lost money for the first time. Next year's attendance dropped, and future Tomato Festivals were abandoned. A few years later, another event, The Sugar Creek Arts Festival, started up to fill the void. I have a few pottery vases on my fireplace mantel as mementos of that Festival.

I have fond memories of Coen's Drug Store, where I used to go up to the soda fountain and buy the best chocolate sundae ever. Coen's was founded in 1892 and continued into the 1960s under the same name. I got many of my haircuts at L. W. (Shorty) Peyton's Barbershop, which was downstairs close to Coen's. In my high school years, I frequented Blunk's Barbershop, where Carl Blunk spun yarns, discussed local matters, and helped me grow up into the adult world. And, of course, I spent many Saturdays going to the movies at the Normal Theatre. For 13 cents I could see an adventure serial, the news, a cartoon, and the main feature. The Normal Theatre is still there but only used for special showings. It is said to have had the same sound system as used in Radio City Music Hall in New York City.

8. My Jobs

The first job I remember having was selling earthworms. You could go out at night with a flashlight and see earthworms everywhere crawling in, out, and over the rich, black, Illinois soil. I had been fishing a time or two with Dad, and we always needed a fresh supply of worms to bait our hooks. I decided that I might be able to make some money by catching worms and storing them in the basement. I constructed a sign, put a stake on each side, and hammered the sign into the ground next to Linden Street where all the motorists could see it as they passed by. On the sign were the words: Worms - 15 Cents a Dozen. I wrote the words in silver paint so they could be seen easily. I don't remember if anyone ever stopped to buy earthworms. I had to try something else.

I remember working for my Uncle Hardy a few times. He always seemed to have unusual jobs.

He once was the Sani-Dydee Service man. Mothers would use his service to pick up their babies' dirty diapers twice a week and return them fresh and clean. (This was well before disposable diapers came along.) Hardy had a panel truck that he used for pickups and deliveries. The dirty diapers would go in a large enclosed rooftop carrier. The clean ones were inside the truck. I used to help him on his route. For whatever reason, I once had to ride in the rooftop carrier with the dirty diapers! (That's what you might call a "stinky" job!)

Hardy had a long relationship with the Laesch Dairy in Bloomington as a milkman. I used to accompany him on his Saturday runs. He took crates of glass bottles filled with fresh milk into grocery and convenience stores, and restaurants and restocked their milk supply. Customers got a refund for each empty bottle they returned to the store, and I took the empties back to the truck. Sometimes Hardy parked two or three car lengths away from the store and left me in the truck. After applying the handbrake, he might grab a crate, and say, "Stay here. I have a quick delivery." I would then be alone in the truck for a minute or two. Being adventurous and car-crazy, I would sit in the driver's seat; release the handbrake, allowing the truck to roll forward a few feet; and then reapply the handbrake. It was fun, and Hardy didn't seem to realize what I had done. Fortunately, I never caused any accidents. I could be pretty stupid.

I tried to become a newspaper carrier for *The Daily Pantagraph*, but all the routes had been taken, and I had to go on a waiting list. Being a newspaper carrier for *The Daily Pantagraph* was about the best job in Bloomington-Normal for a kid. You could make a lot of money, and you could do it all the way through high school if you wanted to. Many paid for their educations this way, and each job was as an independent businessman since you bought the papers from *The Daily Pantagraph* and sold them at a higher price. You could learn how to be a businessman even though you were just a kid.

Since I couldn't be a carrier for *The Daily Pantagraph*, I became a carrier for the *Chicago Daily News*. The papers were dropped off on my curb each day, and I rode my bike to deliver them. (*The Daily Pantagraph* did not allow you to deliver papers on a bike. You had to walk the route. That made sense since the routes had many more customers and the papers were too heavy to carry safely on a bike.) I had a route that covered a wide area near my house. I tried to expand my route by getting more customers; thus, I had to become a salesman.

The worst part of the job was collecting from my customers each week. No one ever seemed to be at home, and I had to make return visits.

The best part of the job was at Christmastime when I got extra tips, presents, and candy. Of course, we had some severe winters in Normal, so I had to go out in the cold and snow. I lost interest in being a carrier when I got to an age where I needed more money.

A high school friend and classmate, Bob Beal, knew I was looking for a job and suggested that I work during the summer at Funk Brothers Seed Company in the Research Department. His father was a full-time employee there in the office. They lived close to me and could pick me up and bring me home at night. The Research Department sounded like a pretty fancy job, but not necessarily.

Funks was a well-known company that sold seed corn to farmers all over the world. They did numerous experiments to perfect the best corn they could that would have high bushel-per-acre yields. They had many test plots all over McLean County, where they experimented with various types of corn and cross-pollinated them with other types of corn. Workers in the Research Department assisted by weeding the fields, pollinating, detasseling, and anything else Funks needed. It was hot work in the sun, and many used the opportunity to get great suntans. I was more interested in protecting my head, face, and exposed arms from the sun and making sure I didn't run into any across-the-row spiderwebs.

I remember one new guy who showed up in a suit on his first day at Funks. Apparently, he thought a suit would be appropriate in the Research Department. He stripped down the second day and looked the same as the rest of us. I also remember that we had some high school teachers working with us. They needed the extra money for the summer.

Also, there was one high school student who seemed very studious. He was always reading books. He had quite a memory. He would just start telling us about each recent book he had read while we all worked in the fields. He narrated the book like a professional and was very entertaining and instructive. I gained a better appreciation for books and reading from him.

I did that job for three or four summers. I think I must have stayed out in the sun too much, though, since now I seem to get quite a few basal cell carcinomas on my face and head.

9. Motorcycles and Cars

1952

When I got to the age of 14 or so, I became very interested in motorcycles. I poured over every new issue of *Mechanix Illustrated* just to read the Harley-Davidson advertisements. I imagined that I was riding a Harley. I went through all the steps in my mind that I could envision to get on the bike, start it, and ride it down the street. I wanted to be able to buy a Harley and ride it for real—not just in my mind.

1954

I enlisted the aid of Mom to try to convince Dad to teach me how to drive. He was totally opposed to the idea. Even though he had left home at the age of 18 to drive a Model-T Ford to California with his cousin, Hobart Fox, to seek his independence, he was dead set against my even learning how to drive. I couldn't understand his extreme opposition. It would take many years to find out why.

By the age of 15-1/2, I was old enough to take driver's training in high school. (You could get a driver's license at age 16.) After many discussions with Dad, I was able to convince him to let me take the class. The course was taught by the varsity football coach, Robert Neuman. He looked like he had played a lot of football. He had a soft voice but could be testy if he tried to teach two or three students at a time. I passed without incident and began my movement into the world on four wheels.

I was halfway through Normal Community High School (NCHS) and in need of some basic transportation. I had just received my driver's license, and I was in search of wheels. My school classmate, Duane Burton, wanted to sell his Cushman motor scooter. (Duane had a fraternal (dizygotic) twin brother, Doyte. I'm not sure it was Duane or Doyte who owned the scooter. I'll just assume Duane.) Duane offered to let me take the motor scooter for a day or two and try it out. It was a standard Cushman of the day, not an Eagle model. It was a red motor scooter and had an automatic transmission. You twisted the grip on the scooter to go and stepped on the brake to stop. Pretty simple. The motor scooter had that enclosed body with a lift-up trunk. I rode the scooter all over town and had a lot of fun with it, but I decided not to buy it. Those were the days when I was trying to decide among getting a scooter, a Crosley automobile, a Harley-Davidson motorcycle, or a 1936 Plymouth.

The Plymouth finally won out, and I left two-wheel vehicles, including scooters, to sit in the back of my mind for the next 35 years.

When I got my license, I immediately started pestering Dad to get a car for me. I had been working and had saved up enough to buy a 1936 four-door Plymouth for $50. (Gas prices were somewhere around $0.25 per gallon in those days. Once in a while, there would be a gas war. I saw prices dip to a nickel a gallon.) That car quickly became an oil guzzler, consuming a quart of oil every hundred miles. People knew I was coming by the cloud of blue smoke that followed me all over town as I cruised the high school haunts. I quickly got rid of it and bought a 1939 Chevrolet Town Sedan (two-door). It cost me $450. I bought it from a used car lot, and I questioned the salesperson as to why the rear end sat so high. He said it belonged to an elderly lady who never put anything in the trunk—my first experience with a used car salesman.

10. Being a Mechanic

1955

I got so interested in cars that I decided, at the age of 17, that I wanted to be an automobile mechanic. To further my learning this new trade, I enrolled in a special program at Normal Community High School (NCHS) called Diversified Occupations (D.O.). Being in D.O. meant that you were not going to go to college and merely wanted to learn a trade. We went to high school classes half a day and worked at our trade the other half and often on Saturdays. Also, we got paid to work; thus, I would be able to afford all the costs of car ownership and also put extra money in my pocket. That seemed very attractive to me at the time.

I was assigned to work for the Broadway Garage in Normal. It was a large facility that had space inside to store 20 to 30 large school buses during the school year. It was only four blocks from my house. The garage had been in business for more than 40 years. The owner, Gail Metcalf, was the son of the garage's founder and had graduated from Illinois State Normal University (ISNU). In other words, he was an educated man and attempted to run the business with new management techniques. He even obtained a franchise from American Motors Corporation (AMC) to sell and service new Hudson-Nash automobiles. (In May 1954, AMC was formed when Nash-Kelvinator and Hudson Motor Car Co. merged. When the chairman, George W. Mason, died suddenly in October, George W. Romney became chairman of AMC.)

As the mechanic at the lowest end of the totem pole, I got all the dirty jobs as I attempted to learn how to be a mechanic. I did all the car washes, oil and grease jobs, the pre-checks on new cars before they were delivered, etc. After a few months of performing these types of jobs, I notified management that I'd like to be assigned to a mechanic and learn from him on more advanced projects. In those days there were a lot of valve jobs and ring jobs. Engines were not as tight and precise as they are today. Also, many people were in the habit of keeping their cars longer than they do today; thus, there was plenty of work for good mechanics, and I wanted to be one of them. Soon I was assigned to work with the head mechanic, Glen Frink.

One thing I vividly remember about the back of the Broadway Garage, where the mechanics worked, was the huge set of overhead pulleys and wide drive belts that ran all the machines such as grinders, drill presses, and lathes. It was a beautiful mechanical marvel that intrigued me. It made music to my ears as it hummed away assisting mechanics in their labors.

Sometimes I would drive up to Kenosha, Wisconsin, with a regular employee and drive a new car back from the AMC factory. That was fun.

Other times we would go out to pick up a used car to sell in the dealership. Once, I was driving a used car back from a nearby town when the car suddenly lost power and came to a stop. The throttle wire had broken. I figured out a way to use some fishing tackle that I had found in the trunk. I attached the tackle to the throttle. I then fed it under the hood to the open driver window, where I held it in my hand while I drove the rest of the way home. That was not fun. However, the mechanics back at the garage thought I had been resourceful.

Several sales people at the Broadway Garage were part-time and worked on commission. One salesman was also an itinerant preacher. Once, when he was returning from demonstrating a new Hudson for a customer, a giant bird flew directly into the center of the windshield. The car was being driven at over 100 mph. The Hudson was a total mess inside with blood and feathers everywhere. The salesman survived but moved on quickly to another part of the country.

Another time, there was a high-speed head-on collision on Route 66 outside of town. All occupants died. One car was towed to another garage, but somehow I got a chance to view it with a Broadway

Garage employee. (I have no idea what happened to the other car.) The car was totally burned out and had a terrible smell. The entire front end was crushed into the passenger compartment. I had never seen a car that people had died in before, and it shook me. I would not see a car wreck like that for another 50 years, and it would change the rest of my life.

While working at the Broadway Garage, I bought two other old cars to play with. The first was a 1937 Oldsmobile coupe. I decided to repaint it a two-tone cream color. Glen's son, Willis, who was home from college for the summer, was a fixture at the garage, and he and I became friends. He helped me prepare the surface of the Oldsmobile, and we painted it together at night.

The second vehicle was a 1941 Buick coupe that I bought from Eloise Craig, owner of *The Normalite* newspaper. She had a huge St. Bernard dog that traveled in the car with her whenever she was out on a story or running errands. The dog shed all over the interior of the Buick. It took me a long while to make it spotless inside. Then I decided to take the body off. I can't remember how I did this, but I did. I still have pictures of the Buick with its body on the ground next to the chassis. I soon lost interest in restoring it. I was now starting to think of other things.

11. My Trip West

As I said previously, I became friendly with the head mechanic, Glen Frink, at the Broadway Garage, who was close to Dad's age. Glen was an outstanding mechanic, and his soft-spoken manner made him seem like a man well educated in the fine arts. His son, Willis, was a 23-year-old college student who was studying mining engineering at the Wisconsin Institute of Technology. He had been in the Navy after graduating from Normal Community High School (NCHS). After that, he got married, then divorced, and now wanted to take a road trip out West.

Willis owned a 1948 Hudson (step-down design) 4-door sedan that was wide enough for me to stretch out completely and sleep in the back seat if I wanted to. He asked me if I would like to accompany him on a trip to Yellowstone National Park before school started up again.

Bear in mind, I was 17, and he was 23. It took a lot of discussions with Mom and Dad to convince them to allow me to take a trip with him. He was well vetted, and we took the trip. It was quite an adventure and one not much different from the one Dad also took at the age of 18 with his cousin, Hobart Fox. I kept reminding Dad of his own trip until he gave his consent.

On the trip, we passed through Sturgis, South Dakota, where the Sturgis Motorcycle Rally was held. The rally started in 1938 (the year I was born) and gradually attracted riders from all across the United States. It would be another 38 years before I came to this rally again, this time on a motorcycle.

The trip included camping in a small pup tent in Yellowstone. We stayed a few nights in motels, but most nights were outdoors in the tent. I remember one night in Yellowstone. It was cold, about 35-40 degrees. I was asleep but awoke to strange sounds outside the tent. Then I heard noises like animals scampering around. I peeked out of the tent and saw a momma bear and two cubs. They had gotten into our cooler and had the bacon out, trying to finish it off. It was scary. Finally, they left, and we decided to get up and get the heck out of there.

I remember traveling at 100 mph and having a Greyhound bus pass us. I was trying to sleep stretched out on the full length of the back seat. By the way, there were no seat belts in those days.

Willis sometimes liked to go to bars along the way. I stayed back in the motel room.

On the way back to Normal, we went to Central City, Colorado, and saw the "Face on the Barroom Floor" at the Teller House Bar.

We climbed a 14,000-foot mountain, and Willis took a picture of me next to a sign with the elevation on it. I believe it was Mt. Evans.

I didn't see Willis much after the trip. Recently I found out that he graduated with a bachelor's degree in mining engineering and moved to Texas. After searching the pantagraph.newspapers.com archives (an invaluable resource I used to check my memory while writing this memoir), I found that he remarried in 1954 and had a daughter, Gretchen, in 1958. In 1975 Gretchen, 17, drowned in Dallas, Texas. At the time Willis was on a business trip to Cairo, Egypt. I grieve with him 41 years after the fact. I know that sadness must still be felt by his family.

12. Crosley Hotshot

Soon after Willis and I returned from the Yellowstone trip, the Broadway Garage went out of business. At the time I had thought, "What the heck. This place has been around for 40 years and just decides to fold when I arrive on the scene. Is someone trying to tell me something?"

My mechanic days seemed to have come to an end. I was, however, able to get a job in Bloomington at a garage that was building fiberglass bodies to fit Crosley Hotshot automobiles. (The Crosley Hotshot was the first sports car produced after the end of World War II. It was just under 12 feet in length.) The garage had also modified the chassis and suspension to give the car extraordinary cornering ability.

I remember going out with the garage owner for a test ride. In those days Illinois had designated highways to have a speed limit termed "reasonable and proper." (This regulation was first applied to horse-drawn vehicles and then extended to motorized vehicles.) That meant you could drive almost any speed so long as you didn't endanger other drivers or yourself. Route 66, which formed a ring around most of Bloomington and Normal, was called the Beltline. It was designed to handle high-speed military traffic; thus, the curves were banked. The garage where I was now working was located just off Route 66. My test ride was fast. Traveling down Route 66 at 100 mph, we went around the last banked curve before the garage exit; and directly at the exit, the owner turned the wheel quickly to the left and the car sailed around the corner without ever leaving the ground. What a rush! I only did that once.

Soon after that test ride, I was told that this garage was also going out of business. My second mechanic job had disappeared. Were the fates conspiring against me?

13. Charmaine

I had never been much into dating in high school. But, since I now had a car, I started looking at the girls I had known for years but never really got close to. I admired many of the girls in my classes. I remember one pretty little girl named Charmaine. (You may remember the song "Charmaine," written in 1927 and recorded by many artists. It was popular at the time.) Charmaine lived in a trailer court on the edge of Normal. Her dad was a mechanic, and the family had moved around some. She was a popular girl, and I asked her out a few times. Suddenly, her family moved to Paxton, Illinois, 40 miles east of Normal on Route 9. I could easily drive over to see her in my 1939 Chevy.

We did the same things other kids did in those days. We drove around and cruised through the drive-in restaurants. We went to drive-in movies. We sat around in parked cars. We talked about the future, what we would do after high school.

I remember the lonely drives home from Paxton, late at night. I could barely stay awake. I had to leave the window down, the vents open, and the radio blaring to keep alert until I reached my driveway in Normal.

Once, I was sitting in my car with Charmaine next to me. We had just arrived back at her trailer and sat there talking for about 10 minutes. She suddenly said in a whispered tone, "Get down! Don't say anything. Please."

"What's the matter?" I whispered back. I could tell that there was someone nearby walking around on the gravel area next to the trailer.

"Please, it's important. I can't let him see us, ah, er—me. Stay down and don't talk," she said quietly. "I'll explain later."

In a few minutes, we could hear a door shut on another car, the engine start, and the car drive away down the gravel road leading out of the trailer court.

"He's gone. We can get up now," Charmaine said. "He's an old boyfriend. He keeps coming around, and I don't want to see him anymore. You understand, don't you?"

Well, I understood, and I didn't understand. Mixed emotions. I thought I was on my way to finding my first steady girlfriend. But he was more than an unwanted ex; he meant something to her. That became apparent when she gradually became more and more distant from me, and we finally stopped seeing each other a few months later.

Years later I would wonder what happened to her, do a Google search for her name, and see her obituary. She had been married (I can't be sure if to the same guy), had two children, and unfortunately had died young (at age 46) of amyotrophic lateral sclerosis (ALS). It was quite a shock to me. I pray that she had a good life and instilled her love of life into her children.

14. Being a Draftsman

Back at high school, I was now entering my senior year with no Diversified Occupations (D.O.) job. I began to panic. I remembered my buddy, Willis, from the trip out West and contacted him for advice. I also spoke with his dad, Glen. Both thought I probably had more ability than I was giving myself credit for. They thought maybe I should consider taking up mechanical engineering and worry about designing cars instead of fixing them. About that time, I was offered a D.O. job as a draftsman at the General Electric General Purpose Controls plant newly opened at the edge of Bloomington just off Route 66. I took it.

While at General Electric (GE), my work location was in the drafting section right next to where all the engineers sat. My job was to modify the drawings for various GE parts that went into GE products for specific jobs. I liked working with the engineers.

I became friendly with one engineer, Robert Whitehead, who had decided he wanted to become an engineer who had a degree. He wanted to study civil engineering. He said that he was moving his wife and two kids to Rolla, Missouri, so that he could attend the Missouri School of Mines and Metallurgy (MSM). His brother, Paul, was also going to attend MSM majoring in electrical engineering. He thought maybe I should do the same and get a degree in electrical engineering. He said that they would have room in his house for me to stay and board with them if I wanted to. Things were sounding more and more promising.

1956

A classmate of mine, Joan Cutter, had just been named Miss Bloomington-Normal in 1956 about the same time we graduated from Normal Community High School (NCHS). She had won a preliminary pageant for the Miss America contest. Subsequently, Joan landed a job at GE too (because of the honor, I assumed). I had been driving her to work with me. A big picture of her had appeared in *The Daily Pantagraph*. One of my co-workers at GE thought he would pull a gag on me and taped a copy of the picture to the passenger door of my 1939 Chevrolet just under the window where I most likely wouldn't see it. Of course, Joan saw it immediately. I was a bit embarrassed but Joan, being her usual calm and collected self, just laughed it off.

I began looking around at several colleges and visited a few in Illinois and Indiana while I was a senior and during the summer. I finally decided that MSM was the best choice for me. My D.O. job at GE and my association with Robert had been instrumental in helping me make this decision.

Academically, however, I was not prepared. I had spent half of my junior year pursuing becoming an automobile mechanic and half of my senior year trying to become an engineering draftsman. I had good grades in most of my subjects, and I was finishing in the Top 15 in my class, but I needed more. At a minimum, I needed a course in advanced algebra to meet the entrance requirements at MSM.

I decided to take a correspondence course in advanced algebra during the summer before I entered MSM. I spent some long hours studying and taking tests along the way, but I finally completed the course with an A grade. MSM then accepted me. I would soon be studying electrical engineering, which required the most mathematics of all fields except mathematics itself. Was I biting off more than I could chew?

15. Annie

Very late in my senior year of high school, I started dating a very popular girl I'll call Annie. She was almost never without a boyfriend, or so it had seemed to me. Annie was a beautiful, smart, caring person. I asked her out and we dated through the end of school and then through the summer before I had to leave for Missouri School of Mines and Metallurgy (MSM). She got me going to the Methodist Church while we dated. We did a lot of things together—strange things at times. We liked to walk through graveyards and look at the inscriptions on the gravestones. Other than that, we did the usual things kids of that era did.

I would be going to a college that was 275 miles away in Rolla, Missouri, at the same time that Annie attended a local university. I would most likely only be coming home for Thanksgiving, Christmas, Easter, and the summer. We had promised to write. But college brings with it meeting new and exciting people you find yourself attracted to. Annie joined a sorority, and that process of meeting new people was accelerated. We soon broke up, as was expected, I guess. (She did meet the man of her dreams at college, got married, and had two children.)

I didn't expect to join any fraternities (frats) as an engineering student. I chose to be independent, feeling that all the fraternity action and attendant social life might keep me from getting the best education I could.

16. Missouri School of Mines and Metallurgy (MSM)

Going away to college was something that would not have come to mind when I entered high school. But here I was, moving to another state, Missouri; to another town, Rolla; and most importantly, to a different life. I was going to get a technical education if I could stick to it and get good grades. I might get a job doing technical things, most likely not in Normal, but in some unknown place yet to be determined. I was beginning to grow up, to be an adult. I could make my own decisions, make my own mistakes, and learn to solve my own problems.

First, I had to find a place to stay. I did not want to live in a dormitory—too much money and too much noise and confusion. I looked at lists of people who were looking for students to rent their rooms. I found one place that was about six blocks from campus. The town of Rolla surrounded the Missouri School of Mines and Metallurgy (MSM) campus. Everything was convenient. The room was billed as newly constructed on the lower level, convenient to street. Actually, it was in the basement next to a noisy oil burner. The floor was concrete painted red. The room, built into a corner of the basement, had one bed, two desks, and two dressers. I found that I had a roommate—I don't remember his name. Both of us had to sleep in the same bed. That didn't appeal to me, but the cheap rent did, so I tolerated it until the guy dropped out early and so did a student upstairs. I requested the upstairs room, where there were two beds. Life got better.

My landlady's name was Darlene. She and her ex-husband owned a store in Rolla. The first thing she told me was that everybody in town knew her so I should be sure to mention her name in any store. "Tell them you're staying at Darlene's house," she said. Darlene was a friendly redhead in her early sixties. Her house was divided in half by a hallway. Her side of the hallway had a single door, usually locked. Our side of the hallway had two large rooms for students with a bathroom between them. We all shared the one bathroom. The bathroom door opened directly across from Darlene's door. Sometimes her ex would live with her when he was sick so she could care for him. It seemed that every time he was sick, he would get diarrhea. That was the worst part of living in that house. Also, it was the first time that I had ever seen cockroaches. They greeted us every morning when we were trying to get ready to go to school.

Darlene let me deal with starting the temperamental oil burner in the basement on winter mornings. I fought it successfully most of the time, but often it would come on with a loud BANG that would wake up anybody still asleep. Fortunately, the furnace never blew up—it just sounded like it would. She also let me cook downstairs on my hotplate when money was tight. I had a good friend, Robert Evans, who likewise didn't have much money. He went out one day with his shotgun and killed a crow, then wanted me to cook it on my hotplate. I wasn't that desperate.

After my freshman year, I decided to look for other places to live. One was with my friend, Robert Whitehead, whom I had met at GE. He had been instrumental in convincing me to come to MSM in the first place. He put me up in his house with his wife and two kids and provided breakfast and dinner for me. The home cooking made me feel as if I were still home in Normal. In other semesters, I lived in different houses. I would sometimes get a meal plan at a local restaurant. I even ate in the school cafeteria a semester or two until that got too expensive.

Surprisingly, I had little trouble becoming a successful engineering student at MSM. I rose to near the top of my class. It took a lot of loans, personal resources, and family assistance to support me the first two years.

The frats worked for many (My second son, Steven, would one day join a frat in Hoboken, New Jersey, and end up being its president.) Being independent, however, was my choice. I was a little perturbed when I found out that all the frats at MSM had files of old tests.

Many professors used the same or similar tests each year, so it was certainly easier under the unusually heavy load of coursework to just look at the expected test ahead of time. I'm sure this is not surprising to most people. It just seemed to be a way of life, one I didn't want to be a part of.

I enjoyed preparing for tests. I would read the book, review all the notes I had taken in class, do all the problems in the book, do all the supplementary problems in the back of the book, and hope for the best. I did well.

A way of life in engineering school was the surprise or "shotgun" quizzes that would randomly await each classroom session. These quizzes were unannounced and brutal at times. You had to keep up with the work or suffer the consequences. The frat boys often did poorly on the shotgun quizzes.

In one of my economics classes, the professor was teaching two sessions for the same subject that met on different days. He gave a reading assignment to the first session and told the students that he might have questions about that assignment on the next test. Unfortunately, he forgot to tell my session about the assignment. On the day my class had a quiz, he asked a question that dealt with that extra assignment. I knew instantly that he had never given the assignment to my class, and I would not be able to answer the question. So, being honest to a fault, I walked up to his desk and said, "I can't answer this question because you never gave us that extra assignment."

He looked perplexed as he reached into the pile of tests that had already been finished and handed in. Then he said, "I see that many people have already answered that question. Are you sure you didn't get the extra assignment?"

I assured him that I had not missed a class. Of course, what had happened was that the frat boys in the first class had warned the frat boys in the second class that the question would be asked, so the frat boys had no trouble answering it. The professor then asked the class, "I see that I didn't even make the extra assignment for this class, and yet many of you answered the question correctly. Just how did you do that?"

Needless to say, every frat boy in the class glared at me, and every independent smiled my way.

Near the end of my sophomore year, I realized that I would not have the resources to start my junior year. When I returned home to Normal that summer, I had decisions to make that would change the rest of my life.

17. Jane and My Year at IWU

1958

I decided that I would enroll at Illinois Wesleyan University (IWU) located in Bloomington. The closest I could come to electrical engineering was physics, so I planned my physics courses at IWU. I was required to take liberal arts courses in addition to the technical courses. I didn't know where my college courses at IWU would take me. I was sad that I was not going to be completing my engineering degree. Lack of money, however, was forcing me to stay in Normal.

I was able to get a summer job at *The Daily Pantagraph*. This job would also carry through the coming school year at IWU. I worked in the circulation department, where I was a liaison to the army of newspaper carriers that delivered the paper locally to residents of Bloomington and Normal. That job consisted of calling the carriers when customers did not get their papers and also handling complaints lodged against carriers for infractions such as throwing the paper on the roof instead of the porch.

I also operated the company switchboard from 7 to 11 p.m. It was an old-fashioned manual corded switchboard with a certain number of incoming lines and then other connections to the telephones in the building. At night, 90 percent of the incoming calls went to the sports department: "Can you tell me the Normal Community score?" I answered those inquiries so that the sports reporters didn't have to interrupt their work. Other times I just switched the calls through. (Little did I know that someday I would be building software to assist in switching calls electronically.)

My work location was just behind the customer counter; thus, from time to time I had to wait on people who walked in for assistance. Fortunately, that didn't happen often.

To my left was the office of the business manager, Davis U. Merwin. Halfway back to my left and behind me was the desk of the city circulation manager, H. W. Stuart.

To my far right and straight back was the office of the president and publisher, Loring Merwin. All the dignitaries who came to Bloomington seemed to find their way into Loring Merwin's office, including Adlai E. Stevenson, Governor of Illinois, Ambassador to the United Nations, and two-time candidate for President of the United States. Stevenson's maternal great-grandfather, Jesse W. Fell, founded *The Daily Pantagraph* (as well as the town of Normal, as you recall).

Directly across the office from Loring Merwin was the corner office of the auditor of *The Daily Pantagraph*, Charles H. Cunning. He was 55 years old, about five feet nine inches tall, and always had a cigar in his mouth. He had a loud voice that could be heard quite well throughout the large non-partitioned office space. (I had no clue that three years later he would be my father-in-law.)

One Saturday while I was working my circulation job, I looked up and noticed a new face. She entered the Pantagraph and assumed the cashier's position at the front desk. That job was usually done on a part-time basis by Dorothy Cunning, wife of the auditor. Everyone else around me seemed to know the always-smiling, blonde-haired, five-foot-three girl I locked eyes with. People were calling her Janie.

She said, "Hi," as did I. I went back to work. A week went by, and I began seeing her in the office quite regularly. I found out that her name was Jane Cunning, daughter of the auditor. One day, she walked over to me and said, "Hi, Wally."

I looked up, smiled, and said softly, "My name isn't Wally. It's Walt."

She said, "I'm sorry, Walt. I called you Wally because my daddy told me he thought that's what other people were calling you. Again, I'm sorry for the mistake. I'm Jane."

That was to be the beginning of a 49-year relationship.

Jane had managed to convince her father to get her a part-time job as a cashier on Saturdays. That placed her about 30 feet from me. She then began taking her breaks sitting on the edge of my desk and chatting up a storm.

We had short bursts of conversation for a few weeks until I got the courage to ask her out. I was going to take her to a new fast-food restaurant called McDonald's that was one of the first few McDonald's in the state of Illinois. I picked her up in my green 1939 two-door Chevrolet Town Sedan. When I mentioned McDonald's and their 15-cent hamburgers, she said, "Oh . . . Do you think we could go to the Steak 'n Shake instead? I always go there with my friends. The hamburgers are a little more—I think 35 cents—but they are so much better." Economics to the wind, we went to the Steak 'n Shake, a tradition we were to keep for 49 years when we were near one. (The Steak 'n Shake was founded in Normal by Gus Belt in 1934. It rapidly grew to more local locations and then into adjoining states. The chain is now owned by Biglari Holdings Inc and has over 550 stores in 28 states. The first Steak 'n Shake in Normal no longer exists.)

Jane was an unusual girl. She had friends all over Bloomington and Normal. She knew half the kids in my graduating class at Normal Community High School (NCHS) despite the fact that she lived in Bloomington and graduated from Bloomington High School (BHS). She always had a smile on her face. She was then attending Illinois State Normal University (ISNU).

Her speech was a bit odd at times, and I noticed that her green eyes were slightly misaligned. I soon found out that she had crossed eyes (strabismus) as a child and eventually had several operations to correct the condition. The eye alignment was still just a bit off after the corrective surgery.

I also found out that she was two years behind her classmates in school. She had been hit in the head by a swing seat as a child, and her memory had been affected. She had forgotten much of what she had learned in the first and second grades and was forced to repeat the two grades. Just repeating the grades wasn't enough. She had to receive special instruction by private teachers to relearn basic language skills. For the rest of her life, she would have continuing difficulties in hearing sounds correctly and pronouncing many words.

Since Jane had the crossed eyes and the head injury, she underwent a certain amount of teasing, taunting, and bullying from her classmates. She tried to overcome all the negative glances and comments by being very outgoing and friendly. She joined every organization she could and got active. She was positive about everything.

Another problem of Jane's was that she had a leg fracture as a baby and had to wear a cast for a while to allow for healing. That slowed down her normal physical development cycle.

None of these circumstances ever affected our relationship.

One night I was running the switchboard at the Pantagraph, and I was the only person in the vast, dark, quiet office area. Suddenly, the heavy metal side door opened and slammed shut as I heard, "Hi, Walt, what are you doing?"

I spun around to my right to see Jane's smiling face. "What are you doing here?" I asked.

"I thought you might be lonely, so I drove down to see you," she replied. Then she did a strange thing.

"I wonder if I can get up on the high customer counter and do a little dance," she yelled as she took her jacket off, pushed a side chair over to the counter, and climbed up until she was towering above me. Then she started singing off-key and twirling around in a small circle, being careful not to get too close to the counter's edge. She was tone-deaf, definitely not a singer, and she would end up proving that to me in a couple of years.

"What the heck is wrong with you?" I said. "Have you been drinking those Sloe Gin Fizzes again?"—a favorite drink of hers.

She quickly stopped and sat down on the edge of the counter with her legs dangling over in my direction. "No. I'm just having fun and trying to keep you awake. It's almost time for you to go home. We can talk for a while," she said.

We continued to get to know each other over the summer, and as I buckled down to a year of study at IWU.

Jane was an Episcopalian. It seemed that the women in my life were directing my religious training. First, Mary Ann, my neighbor and classmate, had turned me into a Presbyterian. Then Annie, also a classmate, had directed me toward the Methodist church. Now, Jane showed me the way to becoming an Episcopalian.

I fully expected to be changing from electrical engineering to physics. So my expectation was to finish my degree in physics at IWU and then get a job in the area. I was going to continue my relationship with Jane as I worked toward that degree.

I remember one physics professor I had at IWU who had been a research scientist at General Electric (a facility out East, not the Bloomington location). He had retired and was now teaching physics courses. He was a decent professor but very forgetful. One group of students had him for two classes. I was in one of the classes. The group decided to pull a trick on the professor.

When the professor was in my class, he started with the expected lesson for the day. About two minutes into the lesson, one especially bright student spoke up.

"Professor, I'm sorry, but I think you have forgotten what class this is. This is the Fluid Dynamics class. Don't you remember, we were talking about the tangential stress on a fluid last time?"

"Oh . . . Wait a minute. Are you sure?" asked the professor.

"Yes, sir. You were going to give us an example of how that worked," said the student.

"Ah, yes, you're right. Let's see," continued the professor, and he went on for the next 45 minutes on that subject. He was quite a character.

However, he was excellent in the laboratory. I remember, quite distinctly, one thing he said that has stuck with me all these years: "Take time to do it right." That's pretty much how I conducted my life from then on.

I got good grades at IWU and learned a lot as I attempted to meld liberal arts and physics together. However, my relationship with Jane was changing.

I began noticing at times that Jane was very argumentative, but at other times she was as sweet as could be. I was never quite sure of what mood she would be in when I went over to see her. Finally, one day she said that things weren't working out, and maybe we shouldn't see each other anymore. I was dumbfounded because I thought everything was just fine. Then, she might call me and want to start going out again. So it continued that way with highs and lows as the autumn approached and the school year would be starting.

I had saved money during the year and was convinced that I made a mistake leaving engineering. I decided to leave IWU after the one year there and go back to the Missouri School of Mines and Metallurgy (MSM) to complete my junior and senior years in electrical engineering. Our romance might be coming to an end.

We were obviously not going to get married. I had seen many students at MSM who were married and living in student apartments. Jane wasn't ready for that and, in fact, instead wanted to go to a school in Peoria, Illinois, Midstate College of Commerce, to take a business course. She had dropped out of ISNU because she had picked the wrong major. She had always loved physical education (P.E.) and wanted to be a P.E. teacher. However, her relatives convinced her that P.E. was not lady-like enough and she should pick another major. So, she chose geography, which she ended up hating.

Jane had been unsuccessful in getting a job at State Farm Insurance in Bloomington but thought that the business course at Midstate would help her get a job with any insurance company. That idea appealed to her. She wanted to be able to stand on her own. So we parted but promised to write to each other.

1959

In September, Jane went off to Peoria to attend Midstate College of Commerce, and I returned to Rolla to start my junior year at MSM. I started writing a series of letters to her, and she responded. Within two months, she stopped writing, and my letters to her were not replied to. Finally, she wrote that she was having a good time at school. Also, she had met someone. His name was Freddy. I didn't see her again until I came home during the summer between my junior and senior years at MSM.

18. My Junior Year at MSM and General Telephone

It didn't take too long to get back into the swing of things at the Missouri School of Mines and Metallurgy (MSM). My classmates from my first two years were now ahead of me, and I had to meet new students. I thought that I would be able to shorten my time to graduate from MSM since I had already taken additional mathematics and physics courses at Illinois Wesleyan University (IWU) that could be transferred with me. Sadly, I was mistaken. There were just too many courses required in the last two years at MSM that I had not taken at IWU. I found myself confronted with taking two more full years of study.

I was fortunate to be inducted into several honor societies including Eta Kappa Nu (electrical engineering), Tau Beta Pi (engineering), Kappa Mu Epsilon (mathematics), and Phi Kappa Phi (scholastic). Several required quite a bit of work as part of the initiation process. For two of them, I had to finish, paint and seal a large wooden emblem that could be as big as 18" high and 8" wide. Then I had to get signatures on the emblem from all the members. I had 75 signatures on the bent used by Tau Beta Pi. (Their emblem was called a bent because it looked like the cross-section of a wooden train trestle that was made up of so-called bents.)

One honor society had an elaborate and difficult initiation process. They held an all-night quiz that began at midnight. This was a rigorous quiz. This honor society had solicited questions from previous members and faculty members. There were no frat files associated with the quiz. Each person taking the quiz was on their own. Anyone caught cheating would immediately fail and could not become a member.

We could bring anything we wanted for references. We could look up anything. However, we could not use calculators—there weren't even many available in those days. We used slide rules to solve all problems that were on tests and slide rules were allowed for this quiz. You just couldn't work together with another student on anything.

The quizzes covered general knowledge as well, so non-engineering reference books were also allowed.

Many felt that having a complete set of encyclopedias was a requirement. I knew that my parents had bought a set of Collier's Encyclopedias, one book a month until they had a full set. We had used them when we were in high school. I called my mother and told her the situation. Could she box up all the encyclopedias and mail them to me so I could use them for this quiz? She complied, and a week later I had all the books in my room.

Somehow I was able to get this 20-volume set of encyclopedias plus all my engineering, mathematics, and liberal arts books, a dictionary, and other assorted references together and lug them to the location where the quiz was to be held. I arrived about 11:45 p.m., found a chair and laid out all my references all around me on the floor. I looked around. Everyone else was doing the same thing.

I had never imagined that I would be sitting there at midnight, half asleep already, waiting to start a quiz that would take all night. The quiz leader told us that we would be taking one quiz at a time on a specific subject. Each quiz would have a time limit. After that, we had to stop and hand the quiz in. Then the next quiz would start, etc. We would get a break after two a.m. Then the next session of quizzes would start. This was to continue until six a.m. Also, since the next day was a school day, we would be expected to be on time to our first class of the morning, or we would also fail being admitted to the honor society. The pressure was on.

I don't recall what the quizzes were. They were hard. I knew that I was missing many questions. I tried to do the best I could. My method in taking college tests had always been to read each question and if I knew the answer or could otherwise solve it, I would. If I was unsure, I skipped it and came back later to try it again. That was also my method for this long series of small tests. But, I knew I was being pushed. My only consolation was that the people around me were also being pushed. I heard a lot of grumbling that these tests were about things we had not had in class. The electrical engineers had to answer questions about ceramic engineering, and the ceramic engineers were forced to answer questions about turbines or laying out a highway. This test was unfair!

We were told that the tests were being graded immediately after we handed them in, and that we would get our results after the two-hour test period while we took a break. But periodically one of the test leaders would castigate someone at random about how badly they were doing. They would say something like, "Mr. Wendell Jones, you had ten questions on your thermo quiz. You only got two correct. What's wrong with you? You'll make a terrible engineer. How did you ever get the grade point average even to get invited to join this honor society? I hope you get better, or you're on the way out. I kept wondering when someone would yell at me.

"Mr. Jake Wilkenson, I see that you're an electrical engineer," broke the silence of the fifty or more people trying to finish a test. "How come you didn't know Ohm's Law for a simple circuit? Are all you guys in here stupid? The group we had in here last year could answer these questions. Are you guys all asleep?" I needed a break already. We were all trying to answer the questions. It was late and getting later. We were tired and afraid that we either would fail these tests or not last the whole night.

Suddenly the bell rang for the break. We had lasted two hours of torture and abuse. I was about to stand up and stretch when the test leader and all his assistants came up to the front. Everyone sat back down expecting the worst. Then the leader said, "Can't you see what we have been telling you? This quiz. This quiz." Then all the leaders reached down and picked up boxes, lifted them up and threw the contents all over the class. "It's a joke. The quiz is a joke. All this confetti you have all over you is from the papers you turned in. We just wanted to see how you reacted to being put under pressure to do the impossible. You all did great! You all are now members of this honor society. Oh, and let me also advise you on one very important thing. This is a secret quiz unknown to anyone outside this honor society. You are never to reveal to anyone what happened here. All you can say is that you thought it was a hard quiz, but you managed to pass it. Understand?"

With a giant sigh of relief, we all said together, "We understand." Then the place erupted with all manner of laughter and remarks to the effect:

"Holy cow, was I led down the garden path."

"We were duped big time."

"I knew there was something funny about these quizzes."

"Thank God, I was failing bad!"

"So who is going to help me get all these books back to my room?"

The colossal hoax was finally over.

The leader then said, "Now get all this reference junk out of here, go home and get some sleep, and keep working hard to get your degrees."

Well, I never mentioned this to anyone—until I just told you, more than fifty years later. Now, please keep it to yourselves.

1960

That summer, there was almost no communication between Jane and me. I couldn't understand what had happened. I hadn't done anything wrong. She did admit that Freddy was nothing like me, and they had broken up. I had written quite a few letters to Jane since I had met her but the future didn't seem to be happening for us. So one night, I took a pile of her letters and burned them in the furnace in the basement of my house in Normal. Our relationship was finally over, or so it seemed.

I got a summer job at General Telephone Co. in Bloomington between my junior and senior years at MSM. I thought this might be a good technical job for me to have just before I returned to MSM to complete my senior year. Perhaps I might even be able to get a full-time job in town after I graduated. I didn't have a car at that time and used public bus transportation to travel back and forth to work. (I had to sell my beloved 1939 Chevrolet to get a student loan from MSM to be able to complete my senior year.)

When I first started work at General Telephone, my desk was on the side of the office where the draftsmen were, since I had previous experience in drafting at General Electric. The chief engineer was a very friendly guy, and he and I struck up a conversation about my schooling and my ambition. He said that I should be working with the engineers and arranged to get me a desk on the other side of the office in a row of desks reserved for the telephone engineers. Unfortunately, they didn't have much for me to do.

I didn't want to appear lazy, so I managed to find work to do on my own in between a few assignments given to me by my supervisor. My supervisor lived close to me in Normal, and he suggested that I could commute with him and give up the bus. Our conversations going back and forth to work helped to cement in my mind that I might like working in the telephone industry, but hopefully in a role that would be more challenging and mentally stimulating than the General Telephone job had thus far been offering.

19. Senior Year at MSM and Bell Labs

I returned to the Missouri School of Mines and Metallurgy (MSM) and buckled down to complete the requirements for my bachelor of science in electrical engineering.

In my last few semesters, I ate at a student-operated eating club. My roommate, David Owsley, was the business manager of the Engineer's Club. He hired the cooks, paid the rent, collected the fees from members, planned the menus, and ordered the food. His payment was free food. That place served probably the best food I had as a student. The only downside was when I was a senior. The tradition was that all seniors in the Engineer's Club had to be tossed in the Frisco Pond by club members. I didn't believe that would happen. Then one day as I was walking home from the Engineer's Club, a bunch of members came up behind me, picked me up, carried me maybe a block to the Pond, and unceremoniously, threw me in the Frisco Pond. Fortunately, the water wasn't too deep. I just stood up and walked out drenched. We all had a good laugh—sure.

While at MSM I interviewed with many companies, looking for my first professional engineering job. I finally selected Bell Telephone Laboratories (BTL, Bell Labs, or the Labs); and after a two-day interview at their Murray Hill, New Jersey, headquarters, they offered me a job. I was to report to work on June 12, 1961.

A requirement for continued employment with the Labs was a master's degree. The Labs had a two-year in-house program in conjunction with New York University to provide the necessary courses for this degree. The Labs would pay all costs for me to obtain the degree. In addition, the Labs required a third year of in-house technology courses geared to Bell System needs. Then I would obtain a Communications Development Training Program (CDTP) certificate and, affectionately, be certified to have a bell-shaped head.

However, I was presented with another option: Get my master's degree by going to graduate school for one year specializing in operations research. Then I would take that third year mentioned before. This option was a pilot program called "One Year On Campus" (OYOC) offered to about a dozen new hires who would go either to Massachusetts Institute of Technology (MIT), the University of Pennsylvania, or Stanford University in California. I would receive a somewhat reduced salary for the duration of the course work. I quickly requested MIT, as did four others including Cree Dawson, who, with his wife, would live in the same apartment building with me and commute to MIT in Cambridge, Massachusetts, for the next year.

20. Jane and Walt Letters

1961

One morning halfway through my senior year, I walked into the Student Union building and noticed a girl who bore a striking resemblance to Jane. It wasn't Jane but the event woke up my brain, and I started thinking about her again. I decided to write her one more time. (As you remember, I had burned all of her letters in an attempt to forget her and move on.)

To my surprise, she wrote back. She had been thinking of me, too, and was willing to see me again if I also wanted to see her. We continued writing.

Here are copies of the letter I wrote to Jane and the letter she sent back to me. No attempt has been made to edit these handwritten letters. They are presented word for word as written. I had just turned 23 years old:

> February 23, 1961:
>
> Dear Jane,
>
> Well, I just thought I'd say hi while I'm in the mood to do a bit of writing. The trouble in writing to you is that if I were to attempt to summarize what has happened to me since I last wrote or talked to you I might have to mail the letter by parcel post. At any rate, regardless of the usual length of some of my letters I hope that I can condense my thoughts to some reasonable length. It is my sincere hope that we are still on speaking terms or whatever you might wish to call it as I haven't wished to completely forget you and the part of our lives which we managed to share together. As a side thought I will say this: in my work this year I have come to better understand

and more clearly realize the usage of the electronic digital computer which many lay-people often refer to as an "electronic brain." Even though the computer will do only what the human being operating it wishes it to do, it still has many similarities to the working of the human brain. The computer stores information in little groups called addresses and then pulls the information out of the storage for usage when the operator so desires it. Although information stored in the computer's memory is not often used for great lengths of time, it is immediately available when needed. I guess most people's minds work somewhat in the same manner. At least mine does. The impressions that were scribed into the addresses in my brain several years ago are still there - not so strong - but still there. So no matter what you may think - I would just like to be able to write to you as to one with whom I have shared a part of my existence and most of all as one who treasures your friendship. The chances are good that we may never see each other again - or if so - maybe once in a while when I get a chance to visit back in Bloomington-Normal. If you could write just once in awhile to let me know what you are doing and how your folks are and all the other things which I know are of interest to you, it would bring a little pleasure to me.

Just 3 more months till Graduation time - it sure seems like a long time since 1956 when I first enrolled at M.S.M. My choice of work has been decided upon definitely now. At Christmas I told you that I probably would work for Bell Telephone Laboratories but of course at that time everything was pure speculation. I have accepted Bell's offer. Part of the deal is that I complete a two-year program at New York University to get my Master's Degree.

Changing the subject just a little - Did you graduate in January as you expected or are you now going to ISNU or what? You know I want to see you find yourself even though you may think you already have.

At Christmas you looked as though you had lost some weight. I guess I gained all the weight you lost. Also I haven't shaved since I was last home and don't expect to until the middle of March in preparation for St. Pat's Day.

Say hello to all for me Jane and if you ever get the chance write me a few lines. I'll not be home for Easter this year so if I don't get another chance to say so - Best of luck Janie in whatever you're doing. You know I mean it.

My Best Always,

Walt

Jane wrote back. This is the first letter from Jane after I had burned all her previous letters in the furnace of my house in Normal:

March 10, 1961:

Dear Walt,

Thank you very much for writing me. I was going to ask you at Christmas time for your address but I was afraid you wouldn't want me writing you.

I was happy to hear you got the job of your choice and were doing so well in school. You seemed very excited about your work and future. I hope you like the east and the big city.

I'm sorry I'm so late in answering your letter. I have been so busy lately getting settled in my new job. I'm working for Metropolitan Insurance Co. They hired me right after I applied for the job. I wanted to get into a company where I could transfer to another city if I wanted to.

Nothing much exciting has happened around here. You asked me to write about my family, friends, and things that interest me. I hope that is all right until something happens.

I finished my schooling in Peoria on Feb. 10. I think moving away from home did me a world of good. I made many new friends. I joined the Alpha Iota Sorority. There for a while I was putting out more in dues than I had. When I was in Peoria I never had a free evening. I'm kind of glad to be able to relax now.

No, Walt, I haven't found myself as you put it. I'm very happy working now. When I get out of debt and have some money I'll be happier, maybe. Time will tell. As I have always said, "May thy will be done."

I hope you have a happy St. Pat's Day. If you get a chance write me about it. I can't imagine you with a beard. I'm sorry to hear you won't be home for Easter.

Walt, it was wonderful hearing from you. Write me when ever you like and I'll answer. Talk about anything you like. If you have something on your mind and like to get it off, write me.

I hate to close but it is getting late and tomorrow is a working day.

Always, Janie

Time went on, and correspondence picked up between Jane and me. Our relationship was back with a vengeance. I was happy, and so was she, but would it continue?

Then I asked Jane if she'd like to attend my graduation. My parents would be driving the 275 miles from Normal to Rolla to attend, and she was welcome to come with them. She enthusiastically accepted.

She did attend my graduation where I received a bachelor's degree in electrical engineering (BSEE).

On the way home from graduation, I was driving, and she felt that I might fall asleep at the wheel so she decided to serenade me all the way back. As I've said previously (when I described Jane singing to me while dancing on the counter at *The Daily Pantagraph*), she was tone-deaf and could only sing off-key. My head is still ringing from that trip, even today. But I felt like we had reconnected, this time for good.

21. Engagement

We saw each other for two weeks after graduation. We had a lengthy discussion about marriage. I bought engagement and wedding rings from Jane's aunt, Irene, who worked at Chadband's Jewelry Store, and then I popped the question. We got engaged and set the wedding for September 2, 1961.

Jane remained in Bloomington to plan the wedding, and I would move to New Jersey to start my summer job with Bell Labs. The plan was for me to return three days before the wedding. We would get married, then drive east to Medway, Massachusetts, and stay with her dad's brother, John, and his wife for two months while our apartment in Watertown, Massachusetts, was being prepared. We would commute together daily to Cambridge. I would work on my master's degree at MIT, and Jane would go to her job with Metropolitan Life Insurance Company in Harvard Square.

Jane had gotten a job with Metropolitan Life Insurance Company in Bloomington after completing her course at Midstate College of Commerce and was able to transfer to Metropolitan Life's Harvard Square location in Cambridge. (Her original goal in attending Midstate was to get a job with an insurance company that would allow her to transfer to another city. Did she somehow know that this situation would possibly come up with me?)

Below are copies of some letters we sent back and forth during the summer while I was working at Bell Labs. Again, no attempt has been made to edit these handwritten letters. Note the change in our relationship. (By coincidence, Jane and I wrote the following two letters on the same day.)

June 13, 1961:

Dearest Jane,

Please forgive me for writing so late but things have been pretty hectic here and tonight is the first chance I've had to write. I called Mom last night and told her my address and phone number here and asked her to send my birth certificate right away. I told her to call you and give you the information too - did she? At any rate we've finally settled here in New Providence which is exactly 2 miles from the Labs.

Did you get any calls or congratulations from anyone after your picture was in the paper? Please write me about it and don't forget the article. Also if you have a good big picture of yourself I would like to have it.

My boss knows I'm planning to be married and I think he'll let me off a few days early so maybe I can get home on Tuesday the 29th or Wednesday the 30th. Anyway, I think Saturday will be just fine—Saturday, September 2—for our wedding. Are we agreed on this Janie?

I really feel like I'm suspended out in space being away from you Janie. I guess that my inner self couldn't figure out what happened to you because I had a terrible dream the other night that you had left me and didn't want me anymore. I guess that my inner self was so used to feeling so good when you were around the past 2 weeks that when I left you, it thought that you had left me, and made up this terrible dream. Being so far away from you leaves me with the strangest empty feeling inside me. It's as if you were a part of me that I left behind. Your love for me in those 2 weeks made my love for you seem insignificant. I don't know what I'd do without you Jane. I'll always love you—I'll never stop.

I've got to run to get this mailed tonight. Write when you can and I'll understand if you can't always get a letter to me all the time. It's terribly hot here so my writing may be a little hard to understand.

Be good. Pray for us each day Janie and never doubt my love for you.

Love,

Walt

June 13, 1961:

Dear Walt,

Hi Honey! How is my future husband? Gee, I wish I knew where you were. If you were OK, etc. It is driving me nuts just wondering. I wanted to call you Friday noon so bad but I felt it wouldn't have been good. I probably would have just started to cry again. Friday morning after you left I had one real big long cry. These past two days plus going on number three have been terrible. Something is missing and it is you.

Honey, I want to thank you for everything. For the movies, the rides, the Pepsi, your kindness and thoughtfulness, just everything. Most of all I want to thank you for giving me you. The two weeks you were here were the most wonderful weeks in my life. Honey, I love you so much and I'll never love another. I'm so happy God answered my prayers.

I took my rings in to be made smaller Friday and got them back Sat. afternoon. I asked Mr. Anderson about putting something (WFK-JAC) in the wedding ring - he said he would but it was nice to put the date on it too. So when we know the date for sure I'll have it printed. OK?

Well! The paper went to press and now everyone knows I'm going to marry you. If only they knew how lucky I am to get someone as wonderful as you. I promise I'll try my very best to do everything in my power to make you happy.

Part II:

It's now Monday and it is hot! I went to the Daily Pantagraph tonight after work and was everyone surprised. Everyone was happy it turned out for you and I. They couldn't be as happy as I am though. If anything happens to you I might as well die too because I would have lost everything. I'm beginning to be a big baby. Do you know I haven't cried in a year and since you came home that Wed. I haven't done much else.

Honey, I love you so much - you are in my thoughts every moment. All I do is think of you at work, home, friends' houses, everywhere.

Honey, now that I have your address I'll send this letter. Remember always that I love you from the bottom of my heart.

Love Always,

Janie xxxx

Correspondence continued throughout the summer. Bear in mind, this was our engagement period. We were taking a huge risk that all would turn out. While most couples get to know each other while they're engaged, Jane and I just exchanged letters and a few phone calls. This was in the day of high-cost long-distance phone calls. There were no cell phones. There were no personal computers. There was no Internet.

Here are a couple of letters near the end of the summer just before I was about to return to Bloomington and get married to Jane.

> August 19, 1961:
>
> Dear Walt,
>
> I sure hope you are all right. I'm so worried about you. I at times wished I didn't worry. If something had happened to you I'm sure your folks would know. I wish you would have called me or written me as soon as you got back in New Providence. Please forgive me Walt, for carrying on this way. It has been over four days since I last heard from you. I know you said on the phone that you didn't know when you would get a letter off to me, but that doesn't stop me from worrying. Maybe it would be best if I just didn't say anything or even think about it. One reason I guess it bothers me is because I'm so tired. The reason I'm tired is because I worry too much. I'm really going in one big circle . . .
>
> Your yearbook came from MSM and I saw it. I didn't know you won a Phi Plate Book Award and a Gold Key Award. I felt very proud of you as I read it. Maybe it doesn't seem much to you but to me it seems a lot.

Love is a wonderful but a hard thing. Two weeks from tomorrow it will be all wonderful. If it has been as hard for you as it has been for me being apart I feel sorry for you. Honey, it sure hasn't been easy has it? Soon it will all be over. The waiting to see each other that is. I want you to kiss me so bad. If only I had you for one minute to kiss me and touch me right now I would give my right arm.

Honey, please write. I love you so much.

All my love,

Janie

August 22, 1961:

Dearest Jane,

I don't know what happened to the mail service because I got your letter dated Aug 19 yesterday and one dated Aug 18 today. Every hour that I must spend away from you is like an eternity. You said that you wanted me to kiss you so bad. Nothing would make me happier if I only could. I am in heaven when we kiss, Janie. I have missed you so much this summer. The way I feel right now about you -- you can expect to get home pretty late when I come home. I want to hold you and feel your lips on mine. I long just to hear your steady breathing again in my ear. Everything about you makes me all warm and glowing inside. All I know is that next Saturday you and I shall be as one and can love each other as much as we want to. Right now I am content to just get home to be with you as your fiancé. Being your husband will have to wait a few days but those days will fly by because you and I will have each other.

The future could hold so much for us if we can make our love the most important aspect in our marriage. With the right kind of encouragement, understanding, patience, and most of all love I can do anything. It will be such a joy to have you with me Janie, honey. I cannot emphasize this too much! Please believe me when I say that you, and you alone, mean more to me than anything else in life. Everything else I do is secondary. God gave you to me and I will never let him down. I won't give you up ever, ever, ever! I have memorized my vows to you from the Prayer Book. Every word has meaning to me. Every word reveals a little more how very much I love you. I love you now - I will love you a year from now - I will love you when we are grandparents. You might as well get used to me because you aren't going to ever get rid of me.

I love your voice on the phone - it sounds so sweet and good to me. I smile as I listen to you because I am so very happy. Honey, don't expect me to be a perfect husband because I probably won't be. I'll do my best to make you happy - I promise you that. My love for you is very strong, Jane.

I must close, my love. Please, try to stay calm until I get home. Then we can help each other to relax with our love for each other.

Walt

22. Wedding

The night before the wedding, we had the rehearsal. Following that, the wedding party was invited to the home of Irene and Forrest Watt. Irene was Jane's aunt.

Forrest was an entertaining guy. He had retired from State Farm Insurance but had also taught theatrical makeup at Illinois Wesleyan University. He was well known around town and highly sought after for his makeup skills in local theatrical productions.

Forrest gave Jane and me a five-dollar bill. He told us to use it to buy a funny gift that we were to keep handy during our married life and to bring it out whenever we had a disagreement. (I think we bought a teddy bear, but I don't ever remember needing to use it.)

The featured dessert that night was an old favorite of the family, English Trifle. It was beautiful to look at and like ambrosia to eat.

We were married on September 2, 1961, at St. Matthew's Episcopal Church in Bloomington.

I hadn't realized just how large the wedding would be. We weren't going to have a formal sit-down reception as happens now routinely. We had a reception line after the service followed by stand-up refreshments of punch and tiny sandwiches. I had not been told how many people would be there.

Jane had friends all over Bloomington and Normal. Her father had friends and co-workers all the way up to the publisher of *The Daily Pantagraph*. Jane's family was active in St. Matthew's Church, Eastern Star, Rainbow Girls, Masons, etc. The result was a seemingly endless reception line (350 people) where we had to talk to each person. We did get through it and a lengthy session of picture taking.

We ended up at Jane's house, which likewise was filled with people. All we wanted to do was get on the road and start our honeymoon. To keep to our schedule, we had no more than 30 minutes before we said our goodbyes, got in the car (packed to capacity), and drove off northeasterly to Indiana. Our eventual destination was Medway, Massachusetts.

Jane's father, Charles Cunning, had given Jane a 1953 Chevrolet Belair two-door sedan as a wedding present. The Chevy was our first car as a married couple. It carried us without difficulty the entire distance of approximately 1,200 miles to Medway.

23. Massachusetts Institute of Technology (MIT)

We took four days to make the trip to Medway. First I wanted to introduce Jane to New Jersey before we headed for New England.

We drove down Mountain Avenue in Murray Hill, New Jersey, and passed the headquarters of Bell Labs. It was an impressive sight spread out like a university campus with numerous buildings.

I showed her the densely populated areas in North Jersey, towns that had no intervening open spaces between them—just town after town with a sign indicating what town you had just entered. In Illinois, towns are separated by corn and soybean fields. Illinois was carved out of the prairie in the mid-1850s. (Chicago was founded as a town in 1833 and became a city in 1837 when its population reached 4,000.) We would have to move to Central Jersey later to see some open spaces again.

Finally, we reached Springfield, New Jersey, on Route 22 and stayed at a motel. The next morning, we checked out and drove to the edge of Route 22, where we observed a continuous three-lane flow of cars headed one way to the right. There was no traffic light! The fast-moving, determined traffic was headed toward New York City or the numerous freeways and toll roads that interconnected with Route 22. We sat there waiting for an opening. We waited and waited, and nothing stopped.

We were from the quiet streets of Central Illinois and had never seen anything like this. I realized that we were on our own now and needed to start thinking like people from New Jersey. Illinois was a thing of the past, a distant remembrance of times slower and predictable.

I could see a slight hole in the approaching traffic. As the hole got closer. I inched closer to the stream, gunned the engine, and made an abrupt right-hand turn into the hole. I heard a horn behind me. The driver must have seen my Illinois plate and thought, "There's a newbie. I'll give him a Jersey welcome and wish him better luck next time." The traffic thinned a bit, and we found a way to make a turn and get to the New Jersey Turnpike. That would take us northward through the network of roads leading to our first home in Massachusetts.

As mentioned before, we stayed at the home of Jane's father's brother, John Cunning, and his wife, Ginny, for two months while our apartment in Watertown was being readied. We commuted to Cambridge via car, train, and trackless trolley to reach MIT first and then Metropolitan Life Insurance Company in Harvard Square.

When we moved to Watertown, we lived on Carey Avenue in a downstairs apartment. It was a bit cheaper. Cree (and Sandy) Dawson, who was a fellow "One Year On Campus" (OYOC) member, lived one floor above us. On weekdays, we drove to the center of Watertown to catch the trackless trolley. It took us to Cambridge. Then I took the subway to MIT, and Jane went directly to work at Metropolitan Life Insurance Company in Harvard Square.

Jane worked until she got pregnant. She quit her job in the fifth month of her pregnancy. In those days, most women didn't work up until their due dates as they often do today.

I found the transition from undergraduate student at Missouri School of Mines and Metallurgy (MSM) to graduate student at MIT to be formidable. (Of course, I was also now married with more responsibilities than when I was single.) The degree of difficulty of the coursework at MIT was much higher than at MSM, and the students were of a higher caliber. Some classes contained military students working on their masters and doctorates.

I remember a few of my professors at MIT in the Operations Research Department. Ronald A. Howard was a 28-year-old who started in electrical engineering, switched to economics, and then to operations research. He had written a book, *Dynamic Programming and Markov Processes*, that he taught in class. He inspired me so much in the study of Markov processes that I wrote my master's thesis on the subject: "An Example of a Discrete Non-Stationary Markov Process." Howard left MIT a few years after I was there to take a sabbatical at Stanford University. He never returned and continued a distinguished career in decision analysis at Stanford and other west coast institutions. Howard told his students to be wary of "mother-in-law research." That meant believing that what your mother-in-law might say about something such as a new product, is a universal truth. You need to dig much deeper into data before you make decisions.

Philip M. Morse, who (with G. E. Kimball) wrote *Methods of Operations Research*, was another distinguished professor. In the cited reference, Morse defined operations research: "Operations research is a scientific method of providing executive departments with a quantitative basis for decisions regarding operations under their control." This book discussed the operations research methods used in World War II to help defeat the enemy. These were mathematical methods brought to practical application to decide optimal ways to find submarines efficiently and destroy them. In 1946 Morse was awarded the Medal for Merit, the nation's highest civilian award for his part in the war effort.

We were surrounded by brilliant minds that had made great discoveries and significant worldwide contributions. I, for one, was humbled and inspired to lift my sights, learn much, and make my own contributions.

I remember one operations research class where students were placed in study groups. One military guy was what we used to call "gung-ho." He was sharp and stood out in the class. After I left that class, I never heard of him until many years later when Cree Dawson and I were talking one day at Bell Labs. We were talking about the space program and the missions to the moon. Cree said, "You *do* know that one of our classmates at MIT has landed on the moon?"

I was shocked and surprised to find out that the same gung-ho military guy was that astronaut. He was Buzz Aldrin. I had completely forgotten his name, but Cree had been in his study group and had followed his career.

I reached my highest level of formal learning when I was a graduate student at MIT. Jane was somewhat intimidated by the students and professors there. She expressed her concern to her mother and her mother said, "Jane, just smile and keep your mouth shut." Jane was a master of smiles already, but keeping her mouth shut was something she had little experience with.

Once, we were invited to a party for all Bell Labs people in the "One Year On Campus" (OYOC) MIT program. It was held at the home of one of the prominent professors in the Operations Research Department. Also at the party were the wives of the professors and the wives of the married Bell Labs students. Cree Dawson's wife, Sandy, was southern born and bred and had an outgoing personality. Jane was always smiling and just as forward and outgoing, although she sometimes exhibited feelings of inferiority. The party started with cocktails. The dinner was Italian as I recall. Over dinner, one professor started talking about his recipe for spaghetti sauce. Jane perked up. Then she really got into the conversation with her own recipe. That prompted other professors and their wives to start discussing other Italian dishes. Jane was pleasantly surprised that all these world-famous Ph.D. holders could talk about everyday things that she knew something about. At that point, Jane realized that she was going to be able to fit into the new set of people that would be surrounding me from then on.

We decided to have our first Thanksgiving dinner at our apartment in Watertown. Cree and Sandy Dawson had gone back to Florida for Thanksgiving, so we had no one to celebrate with. We decided to invite two MIT students we knew. One was Gary Stuart, the son of H. W. Stuart, whom we both knew from *The Daily Pantagraph*. Gary had been valedictorian of the Normal Community High School

(NCHS) class of 1958 and was now a senior at MIT. Also invited was John R. Grindon, who graduated with me from MSM.

Jane had never cooked a turkey before by herself. She did well except she did not have anything to hold the dressing in the turkey, so she used safety pins. When she made the gravy, the pins got separated from the turkey. Some ended up in the dressing, while others ended up in the gravy. At dinnertime, Jane sheepishly told Gary, John, and me to be very careful eating because she hadn't yet found all the missing safety pins. "I advise you to eat *very* slowly," she said. Fortunately, we all survived our first Thanksgiving in our married life and our MIT life.

An additional benefit was the birth of our first son, David, who was born in Waltham, Massachusetts, in August 1962. (David would develop many talents later and use them to pursue a professional career in the arts.)

Fortunately, all went well, and I graduated with a master's degree in electrical engineering with a major in operations research. We moved back to New Jersey and lived in a new apartment on East Front Street in Plainfield. It was only seven miles from the Murray Hill offices of Bell Labs, where I would be working.

24. The Boston Strangler

1963

Between 1962 and 1964, a notorious serial killer and rapist of single women was loose in Massachusetts. The killer became known as the Boston Strangler. The existence of the Boston Strangler put fear into everyone who lived in the area.

So where do you imagine that I was transferred for a rotational assignment in the summer of 1963? North Andover, Massachusetts. I was to work at the Bell Labs branch associated with the Western Electric factory in North Andover. We carted all our stuff from New Jersey to North Andover in a U-Haul trailer pulled by our new 1963 Volkswagen bug. David was not yet walking.

We lived on the right side of a two-family house in the center of town. It was not air-conditioned. We had to keep the windows open at night. The first night there, we were awakened by a loud noise that blasted through our window and scared us to death. I flew out of bed to find the cause and looked out the window to see fire trucks exiting from the central fire station with sirens wailing. We had managed to rent a house one block from the firehouse and had been awakened by a barking code that identified where the fire was.

It was in this house that we witnessed our son, David, take his first steps down the driveway. It was a sight not to be forgotten.

The Boston Strangler eventually killed 11 women. He was finally identified as Albert DeSalvo, but there was no proof of his guilt. Authorities waited for science to develop to a point where a DNA analysis could link him with evidence found on a victim. It wasn't until 2013 that the link was proved. By that time, he had died.

25. The Plainfields

After MIT, Jane and I moved to Plainfield, New Jersey, for a year in a new apartment we could barely afford. The complex was filled with Bell System employees and their families, who had moved to New Jersey from Bell operating companies for special assignments that would benefit their home companies. It was the beginning of the Business Information Systems Programs (BISP) unit of Bell Labs. I didn't know yet, but I would be joining this unit in a few years.

Our apartment, besides being pricey, was fairly inconvenient for us. We had to park in the back of the building, walk around the building to the front, and then walk up a flight of stairs to our apartment. Bringing groceries in from the car was difficult. We also had no control of the heat. The building had a central thermostat. In the winter, the heat was oppressive. We often had to run the window air-conditioner to lower the temperature.

Jane enjoyed getting out of the apartment with David. She would push him in his carriage and walk downtown on Front Street to the Plainfield shopping area. Sometimes, I would go with them, but I couldn't get over how many times we were stopped by people who wanted to rave over David. "He is so beautiful," they would say. "He should be a model." Of course, Jane loved the adoration and attention our son was getting. I, being more reticent, was uncomfortable. (Years later, David would be performing professionally as an actor, singer, and dancer.) Jane was perfectly OK with David's ever-increasing fame. I just had to adjust.

We decided that we needed to move to someplace less expensive. In 1964 our second son, Steven, was born after we moved to North Plainfield, New Jersey. (Steven would excel in sports and academically. He got along with adults well, and had many jobs in grade and high school. Steven would graduate from Stevens Institute of Technology in Hoboken, New Jersey, and become an executive in the building industry.) The North Plainfield move placed us in the upstairs apartment of a two-family house where the rent was much cheaper. We were able to use the savings to accumulate enough money for a down payment on our first (and only) new house.

While in North Plainfield, Jane and I started getting active in the community. The landlord, who lived downstairs, was a member of the North Plainfield Jaycees. His wife was a member of the North Plainfield Junior Women's Club. We were asked to join, and we did. I eventually became Public Relations Director of that Jaycee chapter. That was an interesting and challenging job that required me to write newspaper articles about the group's activities. I would write an article about each Jaycee project or event and sometimes one about an upcoming event. Then I'd take the article down to the *Plainfield Courier News* and submit it to a specific reporter. He would look at what I had written, modify some items, and type it up on an old-fashioned typewriter (the only thing we had in those days before computers) as I watched. The article would then appear in the *Plainfield Courier News* in a day or two, sometimes with a photo that a staff photographer might have already taken. I learned a lot about how to write a newspaper article that would require almost no changes after being turned in. I was becoming a writer.

Bell Labs completed the second addition to its Holmdel, New Jersey, complex and would be moving several thousand people there, including me. (The Holmdel Complex was designed by the famous architect, Eero Saarinen, who also designed the Gateway Arch in St. Louis, Missouri.)

26. Our House

1966

We moved to Freehold Township, New Jersey, in 1966, where we resided on Hibernia Way in our first (and only) house. It was 17 miles from Holmdel and a comfortable commute over country roads. The house was centrally air conditioned; thus, for the first time, I was living completely in an air-conditioned environment: automobile, work, and home.

We had just settled in our new house when we found out that the New Jersey State Highway Department was planning to place a four-lane divided highway directly behind our house. It was to be a continuation of Route 33 that would bypass Freehold but cut through the northern edge of a new housing development called Juniper Farms (my development) to within 50-75 feet of my property. It appeared that this alignment would take out a dozen or so homes also. There was furious opposition to the new road, and a public hearing was held. It was well attended, and no one was for the alignment. I decided that my contribution to this opposition would be an alternate alignment. I prepared a study that showed the alternatives and how a route that pushed the alignment several blocks north would be cheaper. I sent the proposal as additional testimony to the public hearing. I heard nothing, but the state finally decided to move the alignment to practically the same position I had proposed. The area behind my property and along Hibernia Way was then developed as a recreation area with basketball courts, a playground, and baseball fields.

1967

Our daughter, Susan, was born in 1967 on Mother's Day. We seemed to be having a new baby every time we moved to a new place. (Susan was our only daughter. She would one day be graduating from William Patterson College in Wayne, New Jersey, and take a position with State Farm Insurance where she became an executive. She would marry and have two children.)

Jane was lying in bed asleep after she had delivered Susan. Since it was Mother's Day, Candy Stripers were going from room to room bringing flowers to each new mother. When they came into Jane's room, they thought they would just lay the flowers across Jane's chest. When Jane awoke, she saw the flowers and shrieked, "Oh my God. I'm dead!" It took a bit of time to bring her back to reality.

1970

Between 1970 and 1971, I joined the Indian Guides program at the local YMCA. Indian Guides were boys between the ages of six and eight who met monthly with their dads for some father-son bonding. Both my sons, David (Shining Star) and Steven (Bright Star), were involved. We had headbands and feathers and brown vests. We rotated meetings in the homes of the fathers. We went to a summer camp. We also rode on a float in the annual Freehold Memorial Day Parade. The YMCA also had a program for girls called Indian Princesses. It was run the same way with a separate camp except I believe it was a winter camp because I recall seeing my daughter, Susan (Golden Star), learning how to ice skate. By the way, my name was Circling Star. I would use that name again later on.

(Unfortunately, around 2002 controversy developed about the use of Indian names, customs, and ceremonies by Indian Guides. Some people thought that Indian Guides were disrespecting Native Americans. The National YMCA decided that the program should be renamed and repurposed to strip away all aspects that had to do with Indians. This resulted in the program being renamed Adventure Guides. Then it was changed by some YMCAs to Y Guides and Princesses. I understand that some groups have totally separated from the YMCA and continue to operate as originally established.)

I never saw any disrespect toward Native Americans in my group. I enjoyed learning about New Jersey Indian tribes and longhouses.

The original intent was to provide dads and their young children a chance to bond. Dads often miss out on their young children's activities, and this program brought kids together with their dads. I thought both programs were beneficial.

1973

There was significant activity about this time in Community Antenna Television (CATV). There was no cable TV. People used rooftop antennas and rabbit ears to receive television signals. There were only 13 VHF channels and a set of UHF channels numbering 14-82. That was it. One or two CATV systems had been created in Pennsylvania using a large community antenna to capture the existing channels and then distribute them via cable to homes. Other CATV systems were being developed all over the country. These systems offered the capability to receive and transmit many more channels.

The New Jersey State Legislature had passed the New Jersey Cable Television Act in 1972, which opened the door for individual CATV systems to be formed. Freehold Township wanted to be ready with an ordinance, should one or more CATV proposals be brought forth, and formed a CATV Study Committee in 1973. The committee needed members, and five people (including the Township Administrator) were asked to join. I was one of the members. Meeting monthly for a year and in private groups, we issued our recommendations on June 4, 1974. These recommendations were used to frame an ordinance for a cable television franchise for Freehold Township. The cable industry was about to expand across the United States on a gigantic scale. Freehold Township was prepared to be part of this exciting entertainment enhancement just ahead of us.

Freehold's best-known entertainer, Bruce Springsteen, wrote a song called "57 Channels and Nothin' On" for his album, *Human Touch* (1992) that told us what was really ahead. We would be well past 57 channels and growing in the twenty-first century, and many would still say that there was nothing on:

I bought a bourgeois house in the Hollywood hills
With a truckload of hundred thousand dollar bills
Man came by to hook up my cable TV
We settled in for the night my baby and me
We switched 'round and 'round 'til half-past dawn
There was fifty-seven channels and nothin' on

-- Bruce Springsteen

27. Bell Labs

I worked in various areas of Bell Labs as a Member of Technical Staff (MTS).

Nothing in college prepared me for the work assignments I would receive at Bell Labs. A list of them here would probably be boring. Even the technical descriptions might baffle most people. In general, MTSs could expect almost any kind of assignment and most of the time were baffled as well, at least for the first month or so. I would find myself talking to experts, reading extensively, and learning a lot while getting up to speed. Then I would carry out the assignment and get results. The assignment could go on for a year or so—or until my boss might want me to take on another assignment, or my boss' boss might want me to work in another area (which meant moving to a different office in the huge six-story building that housed over 6,000 employees).

The Labs hired engineers who were flexible; that is, willing to learn new things, and create new things. They always expected results that solved problems. You might find yourself doing things you were never trained for, such as programming in a new language or even creating a new language. Examples of the types of jobs I had are as follows: performing radiation studies of the Van Allen Radiation Belts using Telstar data; writing specifications; doing systems engineering; doing mathematical work such as optimizing various configurations of earth communication satellites; performing economic studies of digital transmission systems; creating a personnel system to manage a business systems unit of 1,000 people that had become part of Bell Labs; programming a study of stationary earth-orbiting satellites; building a forecasting methods optimization system; writing code to support an online switching system data collector that allowed Bell Operating Companies to engineer their switching systems; and carrying out a reverse engineering development effort to convert an existing Busy Hour Determination (BHD) system into a new BHD system written in a more modern language.

Let me clarify what was involved in converting an old BHD system into a new BHD system. I was given a set of reports obtained from an existing BHD system written in a language that few developers understood well enough to maintain. Thus, bugs found in that existing system, were extremely difficult to fix. Similarly, if the system had to be enhanced or expanded, the developers would find what some called "spaghetti code" that they were afraid to touch for fear that the system would break. My assignment was to rewrite this old BHD system in a new, modern language that many more developers could understand and thus easily maintain or expand the system.

BHD reports identified the busiest hour in the day for each piece of switching equipment used to switch calls through the office. At prescribed times, say, once a year, traffic data for each piece of switching equipment would be collected and stored for an interval of time, say, 10 days, for each hour of the day. Then the BHD module would be activated to process the stored data and produce the output reports. Thus the busiest hour in the day could be determined for each piece of equipment. Knowing the busy hour when the traffic load was the greatest, engineers could design the office switching equipment to have enough capacity to handle the heaviest load.

I knew all the stored inputs to the old BHD system, and I knew what the output reports looked like. My job was to reverse engineer the BHD system; that is, build a new BHD system in a different, modern programming language and process the inputs to produce the same set of output reports. We would know if our new BHD system was working correctly when our new output reports matched the old output reports exactly.

In 1968 I was transferred to Business Information Systems Programs (BISP). This was a new unit of Bell Labs that assembled engineers from the Bell Operating Companies together with Bell Labs engineers to create a central group to design and develop specialized computer systems to assist the Operating Companies in their continued growth. BISP had a different structure from Bell Labs. The management of BISP contained people from both the Operating Companies and Bell Labs. The titles were different—I was now a Business Systems Specialist, 826, instead of an MTS. The payroll system was different. The personnel system was different. In fact, the personnel system was non-existent.

I was asked to work with an engineer from a Bell Operating Company to design and build a personnel system for BISP use. We called it the Personnel Information Processing System (PIPS). This was something new and different for me. It involved close coordination with all levels of BISP management to create a system that would work for all of BISP and be independent of the Bell Labs system. The system used the Informatics Mark IV file management system. It used punched cards for input. I kept most of the database in my desk. We also kept track of salaries. The punched cards with this sensitive data were kept locked up in the desk of a high official in BISP. When we needed salary data in a report, I had to take my deck of punched cards to the official; he would go to the IBM computer room, submit my deck along with his deck of salary data, and stand over the printer as the report came out to keep it confidential.

While in BISP I created a time sharing computer system to optimally select "best" forecasting models for a given application. I also developed computerized reliability prediction techniques to assist in system design of proposed BISP computer configurations.

In 1973 I was promoted to Assistant Engineering Manager and sent off on a four-year rotational assignment with AT&T Long Lines in the Service Costs and Rates (SC&R) Department located at 130 John Street in Manhattan, just two blocks from the World Trade Center. Getting there from Freehold involved walking to the bus, taking the bus to the Port Authority Bus Station in Manhattan, transferring to a subway, taking it down to a particular stop, and walking the rest of the way to 130 John Street. This commute could take several hours in each direction in good weather and much longer in the winter.

The 9-11 tragedy in 2001 was still 27 years in the future. I do remember attending several Long Lines meetings on the 66th floor of one of those two doomed towers.

Long Lines was the Bell System Company that handled all domestic and international long-distance calling. SC&R determined the costs of providing service and the rates that should be charged to customers. This involved preparing rate filings with the Federal Communications Commission (FCC) and defending these filings before the FCC.

Long Lines had been using custom hardware/software computer systems that the Labs had developed for them. Long Lines wanted to move all that capability from the Bell Labs computers in Murray Hill, New Jersey, to the Long Lines computers at 130 John Street. They did not want to depend on Bell Labs to manage these systems. They wanted it all in-house and under their control. I was to work with the Bell Labs supervisor to arrange for the transfer and make it happen.

After spending almost a year completing the transfer, I learned that SC&R was to be moved to Somerset, New Jersey. My one year of commuting to New York was over, but I then had to contend with driving to Somerset and back each day from Freehold.

I had three year-long assignments in Somerset supervising various groups in SC&R. In one group I designed and built a computer system to track all rate filings. I led a group that used a computer model to calculate the costs to provide domestic telephone service. These results were used as part of rate filings with the FCC. My third group was responsible for rate filings for special services.

The most memorable event in my stint there was the competition created when Microwave Communications, Inc (MCI) introduced its Execunet service in 1975. Up to that time, long-distance rates were subsidizing local rates with FCC approval. MCI had created a private microwave communications service between St. Louis and Chicago that trucking companies used. That service used the local lines and switches for free and then transferred the calls to MCI's microwave service at a cheaper cost.

I was not directly involved in this activity at SC&R, but I vividly remember outbursts by executives when the service was announced and throughout many months while Bill McGowan (Chair of MCI) and John deButts (Chair of AT&T) sparred. The competition had made a huge dent in the way costs and rates would be determined. It was the beginning of the breakup of the Bell System as we knew it then.

Somewhere about 1974, I remember one smart engineer in SC&R who was telling everyone about a personal computer he had built from a kit. I began to wonder if the future would bring these magical machines to widespread use, but who would buy one and what could it do? (Bill Gates and Paul Allen would co-found Microsoft the very next year.)

1977

In 1977 I went to Ames, Iowa, to attend a five-week Bell System economics course at Iowa State University as part of my assignment at the Long Lines SC&R Department. (After the third week of classes, I was allowed to fly back to New Jersey for a weekend.) Being in Ames was, to me, like living in Normal, Illinois, 20 years before. The town was old with few traffic lights. It was filled with students, and everyone was pleasant. Nothing much seemed to be going on. I did a lot of studying.

Soon after returning from Ames, I found that I was to be transferred back to Bell Labs in Holmdel, New Jersey, and would be leaving Long Lines. I had thought that I might stay with Long Lines permanently, but I was wrong. Long Lines was then in the process of moving to a permanent new headquarters in Bedminster, New Jersey, and was adjusting work assignments. Since I was still on assignment to Long Lines from Bell Labs and my four years were up, I was yanked back to Bell Labs. I went back to being an MTS in a new department at Bell Labs.

1978

I worked for another 18 years at Bell Labs in Holmdel, where I had a series of assignments, each different in many ways. Just when I finally understood a job, Bell Labs sent me somewhere else. The jobs were similar to those I described earlier.

In my career, I was a systems engineer, a mathematician, a specifications writer, a programmer, a unit tester, an integration tester, a system tester, and a beta tester. I was involved in both transmission and switching work for the Bell System. I did system testing of high-speed fiber-optic systems. I produced internal documents describing how work should be done. I also went on the development side of the house and built data systems based on specifications supplied by others. Much of the development work involved creating software that telephone engineers used to engineer their switching equipment to make sure it had the capacity to handle peak loads on the network. While at BISP, I developed optimization software and built a computerized personnel system for 1,000 people. While at Long Lines SC&R, I transferred a major computer system from Bell Labs to SC&R and then managed three groups.

It was all mostly satisfying technical and administrative work that I didn't consider work at all. I would end up spending 35 years at Bell Labs (including my work at BISP and Long Lines SC&R).

I decided that I had not read enough great books so I set out to read as many as I could in 1978. By the end of the year, I had read 40 books. I still have the list and the date I completed reading each book. I read *Walden*, *The Animal Farm*, *Frankenstein*, *Huckleberry Finn*, *Little Women*, all the Tolkien books, *Charlotte's Web*, *Life with Father*, *The War of the Worlds*, *The Great Gatsby*, *Of Human Bondage*, *Fathers and Sons*, and many more. I was forever talking about these books to Jane as I read each one. She was a good listener but would never read any of them herself. Not to confuse the reader, but Jane did read a lot of books, but the classics were not favored. She tended to read contemporary books; self-help books; biographies; autobiographies; and memoirs of famous people.

I had begun to write down more and more stories about my life experiences. The next three chapters contain some of these true stories.

28. My Antique Car

I had longed to own an antique Chevrolet. I had owned a 1939 Chevrolet Town Sedan but couldn't find one of those. My dad had owned a 1933 Chrysler, so I compromised and bought a 1933 Chevrolet Town Sedan. The following is a story I wrote about how I acquired the car. I also published this story in an antique Chevrolet enthusiasts' magazine, *Generator and Distributor*.

My '33 Town Sedan

It was the summer of 1975. My family and I had just stepped out the front door of St. Peter's Church in Freehold, New Jersey. We chatted for a second with the rector and then turned to head for our car. Something across the street diverted my attention. "What is that car over there?" I said to my wife, Jane.

"It sure is old," said my eight-year-old, Susie. Not being used to seeing old cars parked in front of the church, we just had to get a closer look. We told the kids to go ahead to our car, and we would be there in a minute.

Jane and I scurried across the street like a couple of kids. As we got near the car, I said, "It's definitely a Chevrolet. Look at the bow-tie nameplate on the radiator." We circled the car like a couple of Indians ready to attack a wagon train. The car was painted two-tone with a maroon top and black fenders. I couldn't for the life of me tell what year it was. It was certainly in the early thirties.

My mind momentarily flashed back to when I was in the sixth grade. My gym coach used to come to school in a 1931 Chevy, which had a big hole in the floorboard. We would have to be careful when we got into the car because the running board might fall down and touch the ground when we stepped on it. This shiny old car before me somehow reminded me of those days again.

I don't know what came over me, but suddenly I found the door handle in my hand, and I was opening the door. I certainly wouldn't have opened the door to a NEW car that belonged to someone else. So why was I so brazen with this OLD car? I guess there is a special license granted to an old car lover to cover nostalgic situations like this.

Just as I opened the door and peered inside at the beautiful clock-mirror, I heard a voice behind me. "What do you think of her?" I turned around quickly to see the engaging, smiling face of Bill Johnson, in his early seventies and a fellow vestryman with me at St. Peter's.

"Is this car yours, Bill?" I said.

"Yeah, I sometimes bring it down to the church on Sunday to give folks a chance to see an old car. You know, this car is forty-two years old and still runs just fine. Would you believe, one day when I had the old car at the Freehold trotter's race track, some fellow came up to me and offered me $2,600 for her. I thought he was kidding until he pulled out a wad of bills from his pocket and counted out the exact amount. He must have been a BIG winner that day." Bill then related how he had bought the car eight years ago for a lot less than that. His son had helped him to get the car back to near its original condition.

Well, my wife and I made one more circle of the car and thanked Mr. Johnson for showing us the car. We left, but couldn't stop talking about the car all the way home. I had been so taken by the car that I had forgotten even to ask what year and model it was. That next Sunday, I found out that we had been admiring a 1933 Town Sedan.

I had pretty much put the car out of my mind because I knew I didn't have the kind of money required to buy a car like that. A year passed, and I occasionally saw the car parked across from the church. I would sigh a little more each time I saw it. I knew that SOMEDAY I would buy an old car, and I wished that it could be that '33.

At the annual church bazaar held in October of that year, my wife saw Bill Johnson with his old car. She went up to him and said, as she had done so many times before, "You know, if you ever think of selling this car, Walt would sure be interested."

To her surprise, he replied, "Funny you should ask, because I've been giving some thought to selling her." Jane was floored! We had always expected that the car would be a permanent fixture in the Johnson family. Jane and Bill talked some more, and that night Jane was waiting for me at the door, with an asking price.

After a couple of weeks, I finally came to an agreement with Mr. Johnson, and I bought the old car, my antique car at last. We took possession on Thanksgiving Day in 1976. There was, however, one condition. Mr. Johnson said to me, "Walt, I know you'll always take good care of the car (he had been afraid that someone else might want to turn it into a hot rod), but I do have one condition. When my granddaughter gets married, I want her to be able to

> ride to her wedding in the old car. Do you think that would be okay?"
>
> I said, "Sure Bill, no problem." I found out later that his granddaughter was three years old!

I kept the car for about eight years putting almost no mileage on it. I drove it around the neighborhood maybe once a month and kept it under a cover in the garage the rest of the time. It had a free-wheeling mechanism on it, and I was scared to try it fearing that I would not be able to get it back once I activated it.

I took the wiring harness completely out and replaced it with one I found in a JC Whitney catalog. It had mouse-hair upholstery in it and a soft top. It had a Body by Fisher that had a lot of wood in it. I had a New Jersey QQ plate on it that indicated that I could only take it on the road for educational purposes.

I finally put an ad in a magazine and sold it to three guys who were headed to the Hershey Antique Auction in Pennsylvania. They showed up with $6,000 in cash, put it on a trailer, and sold it at the auction. I got a note from one of the guys that the new owner immediately drove it all the way to Georgia with no problems at all. And I had even been afraid to drive it across town.

I needed the money to help with college costs that were mounting. I guess it had been a good investment. Oh, and Mr. Johnson never knew I sold it.

29. The Reunion

In 1976 we attended my Normal Community High School (NCHS) 20th reunion in Normal. There were surprises for both Jane and me ahead. The following is an unpublished story I wrote after the reunion, describing what happened:

> Jane Kern peered out the living room window to search up and down the tree-lined street for a sign of her nine-year-old daughter, Susan. It was almost time for the Freehold Township school bus to turn the corner bringing the normal mass confusion of homeward-bound youngsters. Susan was born just one year after they moved to this new house.
>
> Finally, the bus appeared at the corner. Out rushed the usual group of eight neighborhood kids all brightly smiling and carrying on, including Sue. She ran through the front yard, opened the front door, and said,
>
> "Hi, Mom. How was your day?"
>
> "Oh, pretty good. I've got some good news for you," said Jane.
>
> "What's that, Mom?"
>
> "Well," continued Jane, "your dad got an invitation to attend his high school reunion back in Illinois. It's been twenty years since he graduated."
>
> Sue looked down at the floor dejectedly. Then she turned up her face and said,
>
> "Do we all have to go? It sounds so boring."

"Well," said Jane, "we haven't been home for nearly four years now, and both sets of grandparents would just love to see you again. We could take a side trip to St. Louis to see the zoo and maybe take in a Cardinal baseball game. We could stay in one of those new motels along the Mississippi, which look out on the Gateway Arch."

"I guess it would be okay, but I'll bet the boys (her two older brothers, Steve, 12, and Dave, 14) will be so mean to me in the car all the way to Illinois," retorted Sue.

Jane went to the kitchen and fixed herself a cup of tea as she usually did at this time of day. She sat down at the maple table she had recently refinished and began slowly sipping her tea. Her daughter's banter in the background didn't seem to disturb her today. For some reason, she began to think about her own life when she was nine years old.

She remembered the painful and trying times she had as a little girl. She could still hear the doctor talking to her parents after she had been told to go out into the waiting room. She had been a very curious child, so she stood just outside the door listening.

"I believe that she is beyond any help that we can give her," said the doctor. "She is severely retarded as a result of the accident with the swing."

"But there must be something we can do," said her mother.

"Please listen to me," continued the doctor. "There is a fine Christian institution near Chicago which I am familiar with. I know the director and . . ."

"We could never do that," interjected her mother. "We love her much too much to give her up."

"Please go home and think it over," said the doctor. "I'm sure you will come to agree with me that it is the best thing we can do for Jane."

"Mommy, can I have an orange?" yelled Sue in Jane's ear. Jane was suddenly jolted back to reality.

"Sure, Honey, go ahead," sighed Jane.

Jane's reverie continued as she remembered how bad she felt when she had overheard those fateful words so many years ago. She recalled that she couldn't understand what her parents and the doctor had meant. Would she have to go away? She hadn't done anything wrong. She knew that she was having trouble remembering things which her teachers had tried to teach her and that her classmates often laughed at her. And she remembered the almost blank period of two months in the hospital after she had been hit by the swing in the back yard.

Just then she heard the door bang and knew that it must be her husband, Walt, returning from work.

"What's happening?" he said, as he came up behind her and wrapped his arms around her.

"You got an invitation to your class reunion today," she said.

"Say, that's great!" Walt said. "When I was home last summer, I ran into our senior class president, who hinted that something like that was in the works. Do you want to go, Jane? After all, you knew many of the same kids I did, and they'll probably be there."

"Yes, I imagine that Linda Allison, Mary Wopat, and Nancy Bair might be there," said Jane.

"Then it's settled. We're going," said Walt.

After supper, as Jane sat in the living room away from the blare of the TV, she again reflected on her childhood. She remembered her special education teacher, Winifred Farlow, who had worked with her for three years following her accident. Mrs. Farlow had been responsible for helping her to learn again how to read, write, and do math problems. She even hosted her at a summer camp on a nearby farm.

Now, Jane was as normal as any other 38-year-old mother of three. She had married a multi-degreed engineer from MIT and was about as active in the community as anyone could be. As she sat there, she thought to herself, "I'm so glad that my parents didn't take that doctor's advice and that Mrs. Farlow had been there to help me."

The reunion was to be held June 26th. The Kern family began their trip as planned with a two-day visit to St. Louis. Then they drove the 175 miles north along I-55 to their hometown of Normal, Illinois.

The next day, Jane went shopping and purchased a beautiful long satin gown to wear to the reunion.

That evening, as they drove to the reunion, they were unusually quiet. Walt broke the silence: "Are you scared?"

"No, I'm not, but I do feel uneasy about going for some reason," she replied.

Walt spotted the sign for the Country Club and turned into the long driveway which led up to the formal entrance.

As he pulled into a parking space and switched off the ignition, he said, "Now I'm scared. Suppose I don't recognize anyone?"

"Don't worry. We're bound to have a fun evening," she said, reassuringly.

They could hear music as they approached the front door. Just inside, they signed the guest book and picked up their name tags.

Walt glanced into the dimly lit hall and whispered in Jane's ear, "I'm not kidding. I don't see anyone I know."

Just then, Jane's eyes began to sparkle as she said, "Well, I see two people I know. Your memory will improve."

They walked into the hall and slowly—very slowly—Walt began to recognize faces, and faces began to recognize him. Jane and Walt worked their way around through the crowd, shaking hands and reminiscing with their friends of two decades ago.

Then Walt noticed a bulletin board over in the corner with pictures from 1956. He recognized the picture of Mrs. Mildred Kuhl, the registrar of the school in whose honor the yearbook for 1956 had been dedicated. Then, out of the corner of his eye, he saw

Mrs. Kuhl. She was standing across the room talking with several former students. "I guess that she was invited to come back to the reunion because of the dedication," he thought to himself.

Walt felt a tug on his sleeve. "So this is where you were hiding," said Jane.

"Come on, Honey. I want you to meet Millie Kuhl," he said as he escorted Jane in Millie's general direction. Millie recognized Walt at once. She had always prided herself in never forgetting a student.

"It has been a good many years, Walt," said Millie, now in her early seventies.

"Millie, I'd like you to meet my wife, Jane," he said.

"Weren't you Jane Cunning?" quizzed Millie.

"Why, yes, I was," said Jane, a little surprised.

"Jane, I knew your mother and father very well," said Millie. "Say, I'd like you two to meet my guest for the evening."

Millie's guest, who had been standing with her back to the Kerns, suddenly turned around. She was a petite, graying, and seemingly spry woman about sixty-five years old. When Jane saw her, she gasped and then exclaimed:

"Miss Jarrett! Miss Jarrett!"

"Dear Jane, I've always wondered what happened to you all these years," sobbed Miss Kathleen Jarrett, uncontrollably.

"Mrs. Kuhl and Walt . . . This is the wonderful woman who gave me back my life," said Jane. "She was the Director of Special Education in Bloomington. She took a special interest in me and assigned Miss Winifred Farlow to work with me when everyone else had given up on me as hopeless," Jane continued, with tears streaming down her face. "She gave me a chance for a normal life. It is because of her that I stand here tonight at this most special reunion, a happy woman."

The evening ended much too quickly. Jane and Walt were slowly walking to their car arm-in-arm as Jane said,

"Honey, I'm so glad we came. Somehow, deep inside, I knew I had to come here tonight. Just think of the odds of this happening. I know that God is very busy in the Universe, but tonight He took the time to arrange a meeting between Miss Jarrett and me. For that one act of grace, I will be forever grateful."

30. The Scavenger Hunt

In 1978 Jane and I were members of an adult group in St. Peter's Church in Freehold called Saints Alive. We held monthly potluck dinners in members' homes. Sometimes entertainment was provided. Other times the members *were* the entertainment. One such Saints Alive meeting was held at the home of one of the members, Lloyd and Irene Findlay. I wrote the following story about this event. It was published in the *Asbury Park Press* newspaper with a graphic and the headline: "Scavenger Hunt Yields Booby Prize."

> "Honey, it's Dot on the phone, and she wants to know if we plan to come to the Saints Alive meeting at the Findlays' on Friday. You remember, I told you they were going to have a scavenger hunt."
>
> "Sure, I guess so," I said in my usual noncommittal tone. Jane and I hadn't missed more than half a dozen of these meetings of fellow parishioners of St. Peter's Church in the past six years. But a scavenger hunt? I couldn't even remember the last time I had gone on a scavenger hunt. But why not? It might be fun.
>
> Came the night and I was a trifle nervous at the prospect of acting like a kid again, running around from house to house in an unfamiliar neighborhood looking for hula hoops and left-handed toothbrushes.
>
> Twelve couples showed up for the fun, including the Rector and his wife. We started out by consuming eight pizzas and drinking reasonable rations of beer and soda while getting in a bit of socializing.
>
> About 9 p.m., our host, Lloyd, called for everyone's attention. "We have a surprise for everyone," he began. "We had expected to go out on a scavenger

hunt, but at the last minute Irene and I decided to do something a little different. We have made up a list of clues. I'll give each woman a list and she will then choose a man, not her husband, to accompany her on the hunt."

Already it was beginning to sound more interesting, I thought.

Lloyd continued: "Take your car out to Route 9, head north, turn around at the first light, and go south. Look for signs which relate to the clues on your list. When you find a sign which fits the clue, draw a picture of it next to the clue. All of the signs will be along the route which will take you through the Steinbach Mall, Two Guys, and the Pond Road Mall. There is no time limit; but if you are the last ones back, there may be questions asked by your spouse. Oh, and don't look at the list until you get to your car."

I got up slowly, put on my coat, and stood there waiting for 'a date.' Her name was Marie. We got to the car and sat there a minute, pondering the list. "Read off the items as I drive," I said.

"John," she said.

"John," I repeated. "That's it? Just John?"

"That's right," she continued. "The rest of the list is Angie, a stream, a province of Canada, a biblical movie, You-don't-have-to-be-Jewish-to-enjoy-these, around-the-world-in-80-days, somebody's child, Fall gifts, a Shakespearean comedy, and persuasion."

We pulled into the Steinbach Mall first. We drove slowly and peered at the signs. Passersby started staring at us. We noticed other strange cars passing us. Inside them, we looked eyeball to eyeball into the faces of our friends from the party.

"Marie, I'll bet that a security guard stops somebody before the evening is over."

"I think that police officer over there is eyeing us. Better keep moving," said Marie.

"Friendly Ice Cream," I interjected. "Friendly . . . Persuasion. That's the first answer."

We passed the Brunswick Bank and connected it with a province of Canada. I kept looking for something related to Shakespeare, but nothing seemed to fit.

"John, John, John. Do you suppose there is a men's room around here?" I quipped. Marie looked at me in stony silence. I drove on.

We turned into the Pond Road Mall. This place was loaded with signs. The Samson and Delilah sign gave the answer to the biblical movie. We passed a Gulf station. We passed Carpet World. We passed the Merchant's Bank. By this time, we had five answers. "Let's make another pass of the shopping centers," I said.

"I'm getting dizzy," she moaned.

"Just one more time," I pleaded. So back up Route 9 we went. This time at Steinbach's we didn't see the security guard but did narrowly miss running into a group of employees who came pouring out of the store at quitting time. It was now 9:45 p.m.

"They are turning out the lights on the signs," I yelled. "We had better hurry back to Pond Road. There isn't much time left."

As we pulled into the Mall, Marie pointed at the small sign: "Eli's Hot Bagels. That must be the answer to You-don't-have-to-be-Jewish-to-enjoy-these." By then, we had answers for all but five clues.

"A stream, around-the-world-in-80-days, a Shakespearean comedy," I mumbled. We passed the Gulf station. We passed Carpet World. We passed the Merchant's Bank. "These three clues are sure hard, but 'John' . . . that is a real stumper," I said.

"It's nearly 10 p.m. We better head back," she said. So we pulled back onto Route 9 and drove the mile or so to the turnoff. I turned the corner onto Dickinson Street, where our host and hostess lived. "Angie Dickinson!" screamed Marie as the car headlights shined on the street sign.

We pulled up to the Findlays' house, went inside, got some coffee and dessert, and then stretched out on the living room floor, exhausted from the sign chasing.

Our host, Lloyd, sat in the corner chuckling over the answers as he graded the results. Then he called for order and started reading off the 'correct' answers. There was much moaning and groaning from the Saints Alive members as each answer was read.

'Carpet World' as an answer for 'around-the-world-in-80-days' was at least reasonable; but the worst, we all agreed, was the answer to 'John.' "Why, that's John Steinbach, you know, the writer." Even Lloyd had to admit that that was a bit much.

Well, the big winner that evening was the Rector, who only got one wrong. He walked off with a bottle in a brown paper bag under his arm, grinning like a Cheshire Cat.

Two couples were tied for last place with seven correct. They split the booby prize, two giant candy bars.

As Jane and I returned home that night, our daughter, Susan, met us at the door. "Daddy, what is that sticking out of your coat pocket?"

"Have some candy, Sue, and don't ask any questions."

31. Mom

1979

As in all families, children tend to move away from their parents. In my mom's case, I first moved 275 miles away to Rolla, Missouri, to get a college degree at the Missouri School of Mines and Metallurgy (MSM). I came home occasionally especially between my sophomore and junior years when I attended Illinois Wesleyan University (IWU). I had run out of money.

I took a year of physics at IWU and also met Jane who would become my wife in 1961. I would never have met her had I found a way to continue my schooling continuously at MSM. When I was at IWU, I lived at home. My study den was the upstairs kitchen that had long since ceased functioning. I ate my meals in this house. I introduced Jane to Mom in this house. Mom and Jane got along fine.

My sister, Kay, continued to live at home and attend Illinois State Normal University (ISNU). She majored in English and mathematics, ostensibly to become a teacher. She met her future husband, Al, at ISNU, married him after graduation in 1961, and moved to Dwight, Illinois, where they both taught in high school. They later moved east to the Philadelphia area where Al taught at Temple University. Most recently, they headed west and settled permanently in the Phoenix area.

Brother Ron joined the Navy in 1970, and after being released from active duty in 1972, he married Carolyn Purdy in 1975 and moved to another address in Bloomington. Mom and Dad were now empty nesters. I learned later that Ron played guitar and organized a small rock 'n' roll band that played in clubs and for events in the Bloomington-Normal area. Also, Ron would often stop by to visit with Mom and Dad, run errands or help with household repairs. He also kept Kay and me informed when either Mom or Dad suffered any health declines.

We drove home to Normal almost every year from New Jersey. I would send gifts to Mom and Dad for birthdays, Mother's Day, Father's Day, and Christmas. When I came home, many of the gifts were neatly stacked in their original boxes on the kitchen counter, some unopened.

Mom was able to continue her life of being a housewife. She watched a lot of television and listened to the local radio station, WJBC. It was the Facebook of her time. She had a comfortable rocking chair that sat in the living room corner between the hallway and the dining room. The TV was in the opposite corner of the living room. Dad usually sat just to Mom's right in a matching armchair. There were no cellphones, so any calls they got were through a standard landline phone mounted in the recessed telephone stand in the dining room. Either Mom or Dad would have to get out of their chairs and walk to the dining room to answer any incoming call. After all their children had moved away, they used Kay's bedroom as their own. That meant that all their living could be done on a single level. Mom's bad feet and her difficulty climbing stairs contributed to this need to stay on a single level. She was petite, only four feet eleven inches tall. She still had the sweet, gentle disposition she always had when we were growing up. However, she depended on Dad to bring in anything they needed. She did not leave the house much. She did go with Dad and Jane to attend my graduation from MSM. They also drove out to New Jersey once to stay a week with us. I couldn't believe that they would ever do that.

They used to enter contests all the time that would gradually hone in on a winner. They came close to winning but never did. Mom *did* win a cooking recipe contest once that was publicized in an article published in *The Daily Pantagraph* with her picture. But, I think that both my parents basked in the lives of their children and grandchildren, but mostly from afar. Mom was a Bloomington Irish Catholic who moved to Normal with my dad and pretty much stayed there. Dad was born and bred in rural Indiana, moved to Bloomington in search of a job, and met my mom at a card party.

I'm not sure I was ever the best son I could be. I had always wanted to get away from Normal. I guess that's not unusual for an ambitious person. For a while, I thought my working days might be in Bloomington-Normal until fate stepped in and I decided to go to college and a career that lay on the east coast. I was never one to voluntarily call home just to chat. Jane was, so she would often try to touch base with my mom and dad. My parents had never pushed me to succeed. They expected that I would find my own way as they had. Fortunately, there were no bad influences in the home at all: No smoking, drinking, cursing, drugs, and infidelity. They just let me do anything I wanted to do so long as I didn't disrespect them. I remember one time when I was angry about something and Dad heard me say something like, "What the Hell is this?" He proceeded to yell at me to never curse in the house again—I didn't.

But Dad had a playful side too. One memory of Dad I have is sitting on his lap. He would pull the skin on the end of my elbow and say, "This is your chicken," and laugh about it.

Dad was always a mystery to me. He was very laconic, and he hardly ever spoke about his life growing up on the farm in Williams, Indiana. He would talk about his mother, Minnie, in glowing terms yet he never broached the idea of taking a 250-mile trip to see her. I thought of Minnie as another sainted mother, just like my own.

When Mom started having medical problems and I was told that the end might be near, I drove home to Normal from Freehold. I remember talking to her doctor on the phone. I was seated in the dining room trying to take notes of the conversations over a couple of status calls I made during the day. My dad must have had a pad of three-by-six-inch forms used by Eureka-Williams on the table because I still have four sheets from this pad covered with scribbled information about Mom's condition. I also have three five-ring notebook paper sheets with more information. I have no idea why I saved all these pieces of paper all these years. The doctor had given her an isotope test and was reading off the results, observations, and prognosis. These notes were what I heard and wrote down as the doctor was talking rapidly. Looking at the notes now, 37 years later, I can barely make them out, and they also remain scrambled in my brain. My concern then was that the scribbles meant that Mom was nearly brain dead and there was nothing that medical science could do to bring her back. I knew that Mom was dying.

When I saw Mom in the hospital, she was unresponsive. I noted sadly that she seemed to have neglected taking care of herself for some time. I felt that I had not seen her much in her last few years. I had never seen signs that her health had so deteriorated. But it was too late now. Dad had been with her, yet if he had tried to encourage her to take better care of herself, she must have paid no attention. Or, maybe, they had both drifted into a pattern of denial that anything at all was wrong—or perhaps, they had just given up. I will never know.

On March 24, 1979, we gave our consent to remove all life support and let Mom go. She had been married to my dad for 44 years and was 70 years and 11 months old.

Dad was devastated at losing Margaret. However, he had another unspoken loss, a secret that I would not uncover for another 13 years.

32. Circling Star Software

About 1983

I formed Circling Star Software Co. to create and sell software to mechanize filing systems that a user might want to create. (As you may remember, my Indian Guide name was Circling Star.) I had purchased a Radio Shack TRS-80 Color Computer to do my development work. All the programs were written in BASIC (Beginner's All-purpose Symbolic Instruction Code) language. (BASIC was the most common computer language at that time. Microsoft was co-founded in 1975 by Paul Allen and Bill Gates. They had used BASIC to create an operating system for the Altair 8800 computer. That success led to the founding of Microsoft, where many of its earliest products also used BASIC.)

Users could create databases of information that they could use to manage recipes, telephone numbers, inventory lists, record collections, etc. They could then create reports and print out results. I called it Filebox 16. Later versions were Filebox 32 and Filebox 64. The number indicated the memory size of the particular Color Computer.

I started selling the system by placing an advertisement in *Color Computer Magazine*. I even got the magazine to review the software. My users found a few errors in the system, which I fixed.

Once, I printed out all the BASIC source code and laid it out across my living room and dining room floor. It was more than 25 feet long.

I went to a local computer show in New Jersey with my son, Steven, to demonstrate the product. I may have sold 50 copies before I gave up on this venture. This product used floppy disks for data storage. (Many readers may not even remember when floppies were the only storage that was available on personal computers.)

33. Idle Hands

In my adult life as a married man, I usually didn't like to sit around and do nothing. I always felt that time was rushing along literally dragging me forward to an uncertain future. The workday for me was not stressful except for those times when I was starting a new job. Then, it might take weeks for me to pull myself out of a self-imposed depression onto a new level of achievement. However, when I was at home with my family, there was always a need to do whatever was necessary to keep Jane and our three kids happy and productive. Fortunately, Jane usually took the lead with the kids and left big holes in the timeline where I could either be lazy or productive on my own.

I tended always to be searching for the ultimate pastime. I would become interested in something but quickly lose interest and look for something else. Sometimes these pastimes would appeal to Jane, and we would want to do an activity together. Other times, an interest would strictly be mine or hers. Let me count the ways.

Carpentry was the first area to consume my time. In almost everything I tried to do, I had no previous experience, and it showed. I saw plans for a workbench in a *Better Homes and Gardens* book about how to do things around the house. I bought the lumber at Freehold Lumber, measured all the pieces, drilled all the holes, and assembled the workbench in the basement. In so doing, I had no easy way to get it out of the basement and put it in the garage, should I want to do that. (I later did and had to take it all apart and reassemble it in the garage.) I used this workbench for many of my future pastimes.

Next, I decided to create rooms in my basement (a playroom, a bedroom, and a tiny closed-off space I could use for storage) as well as an enclosure around the furnace where the workbench was. I became my own contractor and learned what I had to do from that *Better Homes and Gardens* book I spoke about earlier. I finished the project and then had a place where my kids could play or invite their friends over. I then used the bedroom as my den.

I decided I wanted to become a model railroader. I built a track layout at the end of my new den and installed a small train and cars on an oval track. I purchased accessory buildings and switching tracks. It was a fun thing to do, and the kids loved it. However, I lost interest. I was getting satisfaction from creating projects but not from using them.

About this same time my son, Steven, who had been sharing a bedroom with his brother, David, wanted a room of his own. I converted my den back into a bedroom for Steven. I then converted the tiny storage area into my den.

I decided I wanted to become an amateur radio operator (ham). (I had also had this calling before I went to college and studied up to take the test to get my license; however, I didn't have the resources to complete the task at that time.) What I needed was a ham radio. I saw a kit in the Heathkit catalog, ordered it, and spent a good month putting it together. The kit included a book with steps to follow. You had to solder every connection, it seemed. Make a mistake, and nothing would work, or you would see smoke rising out of your uncompleted kit. I was lucky and got the radio to work. I then studied the American Radio Relay League (ARRL) manual and took the novice test to get my first license. My call sign was WN2CAR. (The N stood for novice.) I could only send Morse code with that license. If I wanted to use voice, I had to pass another test and get the next higher license.

So I had my radio that I assembled myself from a kit, and I had my license, but I did not have an outside antenna to connect to the radio. I fastened together four 8-foot sections of two-by-fours with bolts to make a nearly 30-foot pole. One end section of the pole was then attached with bolts to the 4x4 inside corner post of the wooden fence around my pool. I strung an antenna wire from the top of that pole all the way to the top edge of the roof over my garage. Then I connected a lead-in wire to the center of the antenna wire to create a dipole antenna and ran that wire to the top of the outside back wall of my house. It then ran down the rear wall to a position where a hole could be drilled through the siding into the crawl space in my basement. I then ran the lead-in wire through the crawl space into the ceiling of my basement den and dropped the lead-in wire into the den and attached it to the ham radio. Unbelievably, this setup worked, and I was able to send Morse code to several people in the United States and get responses back. At that point, all the technical aspects were working. All I had to do then was practice my code to bring my speed up so I could take the next test to be able to talk over the radio. At that point, I lost interest. I eventually took the antenna system down. (My neighbors were already wondering what I was building on my house.)

At one time I bought an antique car (my '33 Chevy Town Sedan discussed earlier). I liked working on it, but I wasn't getting any satisfaction from owning it. When I needed money to keep my kids in college, I sold it for twice what I had paid for it. I then had half of my garage back again so I disassembled the workbench in the basement and reassembled it on that side of my garage, allowing just enough space to drive a second car into the garage.

In 1988 we took up skiing for a year. Jane's sister Carol and her husband Jack had visited us and told of their love for the sport. They convinced us to give it a try starting at Jack Frost/Big Boulder Ski Resorts in Lake Harmony, Pennsylvania. We took ski lessons and rented equipment. Later we bought our own equipment. We took about a dozen trips to ski resorts in Pennsylvania, New Jersey, New York, Connecticut, and Massachusetts. We even took one family ski vacation. Skiing was fun, but we never got very good at it. I lost interest in skiing the first time I saw a motorcyclist ride into a ski resort with skis on the back of his bike. I thought the motorcycle was way more cool!

I was always interested in computers. I started using the big IBM mainframes in 1961 at Bell Labs. It wasn't until the 1980s that I got a personal computer. I was one of the first to use an America Online (AOL) account. I built a single-line computer bulletin board system (BBS) and communicated with my paperboy, Tom, who lived two blocks away and had done the same thing. (He eventually received multiple college degrees in both engineering and business, got married, had two children, and currently is Vice President and Chief Information Officer for a large southeastern hospital.) I was creating websites in the late 1990s that would be beneficial to me in a few years.

I became interested in genealogy when I began investigating my own family tree. At that time, I had to go to libraries or county and city records to find information. Then computers and genealogical software evolved, allowing me to search online. Genealogy has continued to be an interest that would prove beneficial later.

In 1989 my quest for a lasting pastime ended. At the age of 51, I decided I wanted to learn to ride a motorcycle. I had caught the "motorcycle bug." From then on, motorcycles would be a central part of my life (and Jane's). Writing about motorcycles would become a passion, too.

34. Motorcycles

1989

Jane and I began riding motorcycles in 1989. We were both 51 years old—pretty late in life to take up what most people thought was a dangerous sport.

Two men named Jack gave me the push I needed to get started. Surprisingly, Jane wanted to learn to ride also.

The first Jack was Jane's brother-in-law, Jack Aldridge, who had gotten us interested in skiing the previous year. Jack lived in my hometown, Normal, and his sister (Kay Baylor) was my next-door neighbor. (You may recall Mrs. Baylor cared for my sister and me when Dad had to take a trip to Peoria.) Both Jack and his wife rode BMW motorcycles, and I envied them and their machines every time I returned home for a visit. Jack had a well-equipped machine shop garage, and I listened intently when he talked about his bikes and how he maintained them.

Jack Mac Phee of New Jersey was the other Jack. He kick-started my process of learning how to ride by introducing me to a group of Honda Gold Wing riders who would continue to encourage both my wife and me in our lifelong adventure in motorcycling.

Jane once wrote about Jack Mac Phee and thanked him publicly for his role in getting us started. I'll let her words express how much influence Jack had on us:

> "Walt met Jack at Bell Laboratories in 1989. Walt and I had decided to take up motorcycling. Both of us wanted to learn all we could. Walt found out that the Labs had a motorcycle club that met during the lunch hour. He went to one of their meetings and met Jack, who was the chairman. Jack quickly assumed the role of mentor and initiated regular discussions

about every aspect of motorcycling. He suggested that we take a Motorcycle Safety Foundation (MSF) class at a nearby college.

Soon after this, both Walt and I passed the MSF beginners course. We had only one bike so it was decided that Walt would get his license first. To practice, you needed someone to ride with you who already had their license. Jack was our guy.

Jack would come by on his motorcycle and ask if Walt would like to go for a ride to get practice. One time I was standing in the driveway, and Jack asked me if I would like to ride too. Of course, I said I would love to and hopped onto the back of his motorcycle. He took us through the back roads of Monmouth County. I can still remember seeing the chipmunks running along the road while I was sitting on the back of Jack's bike. That ride introduced me to a nature that I had never experienced before.

When it came time for Walt to take his riding test, it was Jack who went with him. It was a very rainy day. On the way, Jack came upon deep standing water in the road and tried to stop but ended up turning his bike over and skidding. I heard that even sparks were flying. Once they got Jack's bike upright, they continued to the testing facility where Walt was told he did not have a correct insurance card and could not take the test. Jack was very nice to ride over with him on another date so he could finally take the test and pass it. In the spring, I took the test also and passed it.

Time went by. Jack met Val and kept telling us he had met this wonderful lady at his church. At that time, I was riding a Honda Pacific Coast, and Walt

> was riding a Honda Gold Wing so I wanted to join the Gold Wing Road Riders Association (GWRRA). Jack and Val kept asking us to join the local chapter of GWRRA, just four miles away. Finally, when I got a trike (a three-wheel motorcycle), we decided to join the chapter. That has led to many years of motorcycle adventures with chapter members taking us to places we would never have thought to go in a car. Motorcycling has become a big part of our lives now.
>
> We appreciate all Jack has done for us in helping us to begin to ride motorcycles. He went the extra mile to take us under his wing and introduce us to a new way of living through Fun, Safety, and Knowledge. Thank You, Jack. -- Jane Ann Kern"

1991

Both Jane and I rode a 1981 Honda CM400T motorcycle as our first bike. Jane then bought a 1989 Honda Shadow 600, and I purchased a 1991 Honda Nighthawk 750. A few months later I had my first incident on the Nighthawk.

As you may know, riding a motorcycle to work can often take twice as long as driving a car. How can that be? Simple. With a bike, sometimes it has a mind of its own. It sees a corner coming up and then automatically activates the turn signal. That's your signal that the bike wants to take you to work using a different, more scenic, and perhaps more challenging route. It happened to me.

I was riding to work along Route 537 east in the Colts Neck, New Jersey, area when the bike suddenly slowed, flipped on the right turn signal, and honked once to get my attention. I complied and awaited a new adventure. I knew that the road I had turned onto was the road to an old abandoned airport. The sun was out, the air was flowing past my helmet, and I was relaxed, enjoying the ride. All of a sudden,

I felt a sharp pain on the left side of my neck. I instantly knew that something had stung me. I didn't think much about it, but suddenly I began to feel lightheaded.

The bee sting reacted quickly, and I was forced to stop on the narrow gravel road, turn around, and head back to Route 537 thinking all the time, "Where do I go?" All I could think of was the Colts Neck Rescue Squad that I knew to be nearby.

I rode the bike straight to the Rescue Squad building hoping I wouldn't pass out or get too dizzy to balance the bike. I got to the building, got off the bike, and ran to the first door I saw. It was locked. It didn't occur to me that there wouldn't be anyone there. I tried another door, and it opened. A clanging bell went off as I entered the building. I was an intruder.

Almost immediately I heard a disembodied voice call out, "Who are you? What are you doing here? What's your name?" I answered as best I could in my steadily increasing dizziness and told them what happened. The voice quickly answered, "I'll dispatch an ambulance. Stay where you are. Sit down, so you won't hurt yourself."

I told the voice that I was on a motorcycle and asked what I should do with it. I was told that someone would move it into the building when the ambulance came. I could come back later and get the bike.

Within a few minutes, the rescue squad arrived, stabilized me, and transported me to Freehold Area Hospital. I had never been involved as a patient being transported to the hospital. The siren was going. I was still quite alert.

When we arrived at the Emergency entrance, I was taken in and expedited through to a treatment area—no waiting involved. They called Jane and informed her. She came right over. I was administered a shot of adrenalin (epinephrine), and that's all it took to get me released.

I called into work and told my supervisor the situation. I stayed home the rest of the day and actually went back to the Colts Neck Rescue building before sunset, got my bike, and rode home with no problem.

I was required by the doctor to get one of those rescue pens and always carry it with me. (I didn't think I needed it, but I kept up an annual renewal for more than ten years without ever using it.)

After I had got the bike home and it was just the bike and me in the garage, I proceeded to chew the bike out for giving me such terrible advice on my trip to work. The bike never again suggested that I make that turn on any trip I took to work. I traded it in on a Honda PC800 in a few years. The PC800 always let me decide what turns I wanted to make on my trips.

35. Dad

My mother, Margaret, had died on March 24, 1979, at the age of 70. On March 1, 1982, almost three years later, I got a handwritten letter from Dad. Here is that letter, word for word with no editing:

> Mar 1 - 1982
>
> Dear Son and Family
>
> I am OK and hope you are all well.
>
> Got all that snow out of the way. It missed us. We didn't get over 5 in. so far this winter.
>
> I would like to make a change in our Loan. I want to make it a Gift for college expense. I will Return what you have paid back, and I will feel I have Done a Good Deed for Education.
>
> Hope you can read my Writing. Will write more next time.
>
> Dad

I knew I had student loans to repay. I have forgotten how much I borrowed and how much I repaid, but I saw a completely new side of Dad. At 74 years of age, he had returned all the money I paid back and also forgiven the loan. I had never seen this altruistic side of him.

He would live in his house on Linden Street another seven years. He did his own cooking. When his vision deteriorated and he lost his sense of smell, it was no longer safe for him to be alone. (My brother, Ron, told me that Dad had fallen over the gas stove once and burned his face.) Dad would spend the next four years in a nursing home. Ron and his wife, Carolyn, visited him frequently and kept Kay and me updated as his health continued to decline.

On May 18, 1992, my father died. He was 84 years old. Doctors said his heart was strong, and he could have lived a few more years had he not contracted pneumonia.

However, Dad had many secrets that he never discussed with his children. I'll have more to say about this later.

My sister, Kay, flew in from Arizona for the funeral, and I came from New Jersey. Alone in the house where we had spent our childhood, we sadly became aware that our one direct link to the past had slipped away. We were soon to discover that Dad had died holding on to secrets that haunted him most of his life—secrets he had never told anyone, perhaps not even our mother.

The funeral service was held at the Stubblefield Funeral Home in Normal, the same place we used for Mom's funeral 14 years earlier. I stood in the back, greeting family, friends, and other locals who had read the obituary in *The Daily Pantagraph.* I saw several kids (now in their mid-fifties) who had been in my graduating class at Normal Community High School (NCHS). Some like Dick Huffington, my boyhood pal, knew my parents well and expressed their condolences. Then we started recalling our high school days—the good times and the bad times. Jokes and laughter broke out as if we were at a high school reunion. I was concerned that we were being a bit too loud for such a solemn occasion. It's certainly true that funerals bring together longtime friends and family, but the good feelings engendered at these sad gatherings are not lasting. Since then, I have not seen or talked to Dick for nearly a quarter century.

Dad's mother, Minnie, had died 41 years ago, when I was 13 years old, but we never attended Minnie's funeral. I don't think the subject ever came up in my house. I was able to recover a four-page scribbled letter from Minnie, addressed to Dad during World War

II. I think it shows a mother's concern for her son and his family and her need to stay connected in any way she could during a wartime situation for which no one knew the outcome. Here is that letter, transcribed the best I could, exhibiting Minnie's limited ability to write yet demonstrating her deep love for her son. (The letter has not been edited or corrected for spelling.)

> Oct 12, 1942
>
> My Dear son family
>
> I will try and write you a few lines this letter finds you all well as you could Be expected to Be. hoping to find you All well find and dandy Well I guess you herd that Raymond Had gone to the Armie he has Bin In over a month I went to Bedford Saturday and stayed At Blanches all night and Raymond was there 5 o'clock Sunday morning and left 11:15 Back to Camp Grant Ill. I'm worried Bout you and your family I think it wouldn't hurt you to write and send me your Picture of you and your family. all of the rest of the children have give me there pictures I want yours Time is getting awful Bad I would like to here from all you kids Will Close hoping to here from you. Your mother to son
>
> Minnie Lee Kern

Life went on after that, but big secrets lay ahead.

36. I Ride on "20/20"

1993

June 11, 1993

I was sitting on my couch watching an episode of "20/20" on television. At that point, I was riding a 1990 Honda Pacific Coast (PC800) motorcycle.

There was a segment called "Until They Have Answers." It was happening in New Jersey associated with the Naval Weapons Station Earle base that had an entrance gate on Route 34 in Colts Neck, New Jersey.

I had previously recorded this program that same day and was watching it on my Video Cassette Recorder (VCR). The program had shifted to that entrance gate, and the reporter was about to interview someone. But before the interview started, the camera was showing Route 34 and the traffic rushing past. Suddenly, a red motorcycle passed across the screen. It was only on for a few seconds. I yelled to Jane, "That looks like me riding my PC800!" I quickly backed up the tape and replayed it in slow motion. It was me, for sure.

Then, I remembered the day I had taken my red 1990 Honda PC800 out for a short spin. I rode out Route 537 east from Freehold to Route 34, turned right to go south on 34 and just enjoyed the ride on that pleasant spring day. As I approached the Naval Weapons Station Earle gate area, I saw several cars and trucks parked on the side of the road. I slowed down just a little. I saw photographers with video cameras scanning the highway and gate. I passed by and continued on my way. This had only been a few weeks before I was to watch that ABC "20/20" show. It *was* me in the television segment.

That was the only time I ever appeared on a nationally televised highly-rated show. I even ordered an ABC "20/20" videotape of that segment to have as a permanent trophy of that auspicious and memorable ride.

37. First Tour

I wrote the following story about a motorcycle trip that Jane and I took in 1993. It was our first long motorcycle ride cross-country. It also explains how we got into motorcycling. This story is also contained in my fourth book, *Motorcycle Kick-Starts*.

> "Remember When Motorcycles Were Dangerous and Sex Was Safe?" This '90s truism was emblazoned across the T-shirt worn by our friend Carmela as we sat in a restaurant in Lewes, Delaware, on Halloween, 1992. My wife, Jane, and I had ridden down to Lewes from New Jersey on our motorcycles to attend a Polar Bear Grand Tour meeting. We were new to motorcycling having only taken up the sport four years ago after we had entered our fifties. We started out by taking a course sponsored by the Motorcycle Safety Foundation. It was a rapid progression from obtaining our licenses to Jane's joining a women's riding club—the Spokes-Women—to taking longer rides, to attending out-of-state rallies, and most recently, joining the AMA-sponsored Polar Bear Grand Tour that rode every Sunday throughout the winter.
>
> Carmela had ridden down with us. We sat there talking about how rapidly Jane and I had immersed ourselves in motorcycling. Carmela leaned over to me and said, "I'm planning to ride out to Cody, Wyoming, next August to attend a rally. Want to come along?" Well, we had gone to several rallies as far away as Lancaster, Pennsylvania, a distance of 130 miles, but Cody was an unfathomable 2,500 miles away! The suggestion, however, did strike a chord somewhere within me, and I began to ponder the consequences and the pitfalls of such a journey.

Jane and I were neophytes at motorcycling, and we didn't even have bikes that were designed for long-distance travel. It wasn't long before we made the decision to make the trip and began in earnest to plan for the adventure. I told Jane, "If we survive this trip, we'll either want to keep doing it or never want to go again."

We purchased two identical 1990 Honda Pacific Coast motorcycles in November and used them throughout the rest of the Polar Bear riding season. We plotted out our course west and realized that two other significant events would be taking place during our travel time: The Black Hills Motor Classic held at Sturgis, South Dakota, and the 150th anniversary of the Oregon Trail. As it turned out, we also had to contend with the flooding in the Midwest.

As the time neared to start our journey, Carmela had decided to drop out, but another couple, Harry and Donna, and our good friend Warren had decided to join us. Our caravan was to consist of four motorcycles and five people. Our ground rules were few. We would stop every hundred miles to get gas and take a break. We would ride until about 5 p.m. and then look for a motel. We would travel the interstates to make time because our primary goal was to sightsee in the South Dakota and Wyoming areas. I had one goal: get to Cody. Jane had another goal: get to the Grand Teton Mountains south of Yellowstone Park.

We began our adventure August 7 on a foggy, misty morning traveling down I-195 to meet our companions at the first rest stop on the New Jersey Turnpike. We rode hard the first two days and arrived weary in our hometown of Normal, Illinois, 900 miles from New Jersey.

We stayed at the home of Jane's sister, Carol. It was Carol and her husband, Jack, who were the inspiration for my making the original decision to take up motorcycling. We had listened to their many motorcycle stories over the years on visits to Illinois and spent many evenings looking longingly at their classic BMW motorcycles. Finally, four years ago, I asked Jane if she would like to learn to ride, and her enthusiastic "yes" response started us down the path that had led to this trip. One of my dreams was to see Jane and her sister ride their motorcycles together. That dream was soon realized on the third day of our adventure as they took a 50-mile ride through the Illinois countryside.

On the next day, we left Illinois and crossed the Mississippi River at Davenport, Iowa. We witnessed the fury of that mighty river firsthand. Next came the flooded area at Des Moines, Iowa, where people were still trying to put their lives back together.

Soon we were in Nebraska and found ourselves close to the original Oregon Trail, where thousands of settlers had surmounted incredible odds to make new homes in the West. We stopped in the little town of Dannebrog, Nebraska, population 350, made famous by the monthly television report, "Postcards from Nebraska," by Roger Welsch on CBS News Sunday Morning.

Jane went into a tiny cafe called the "Drive Inn" on the edge of town to use the bathroom. She walked in and asked if they had a public restroom. The proprietor said, "No, but you can go right back through the kitchen and use our bathroom."

Jane said, "Are you serious? I don't want to impose." The proprietor insisted. After Jane had returned, she said, "You know, you are all famous. I watch all the stories about Dannebrog on TV."

The proprietor replied, "Did you see that last show about the ice cream social? My wife made the ice cream."

Jane said, "I also saw the segment about the potato soup contest. They said they ran out of potatoes in town because everybody was making potato soup."

"Yeah," said the proprietor, "My wife won third place in that."

Jane felt welcome in Dannebrog and couldn't stop talking about the people she met there.

We traveled on Route 2 through the Sand Hills region of Nebraska heading northwest toward South Dakota. This region was my personal favorite. We probably saw 10 cars in 50 miles—such a pleasure coming from New Jersey—and we just spread out our bikes and looked all around at the beautiful rolling horse and cattle ranches, the clear blue streams and lakes, and occasional 100-car coal trains heading East from Wyoming.

We encountered only one bad motel experience on the trip. It occurred in a tiny town in Nebraska. The only motel in town was operated out of a gas station. The room had a door without a lock, a 10-inch black-and-white TV with three flickering channels, a bathroom fixture turned on and off using a wrench, and numerous bugs. When Jane turned down the bedspread, a grasshopper jumped out. "We are sleeping in the same bed tonight," she said. "If anything bites me, it's going to bite you too."

On the next day, we passed into South Dakota and headed toward Mount Rushmore. We stayed in the Rapid City area for the next four days enjoying the sights of Mount Rushmore, Custer State Park, the Badlands, and Sturgis.

About this time, our group decided to split up. Harry and Donna decided to pursue the Glacier National Park region while Warren, Jane, and I would stick together.

We were told that Sturgis hosted more than 200,000 motorcyclists during this, its fifty-third year. Jane was excited as I led the group into Sturgis and turned down Main Street.

In reality, motorcyclists could be found everywhere within an 80-mile radius of Sturgis. We saw motorcyclists on every road forming long caravans in both directions.

The town of Deadwood had a marked-off area downtown for motorcycles, and there were thousands of bikes there. Mount Rushmore was similarly inundated. Even the Wall Drugstore and the Badlands, more than 70 miles away, were saturated with riders.

At Sturgis and throughout its environs, motorcycles were ubiquitously present, and automobiles were in the minority. Originally, we only expected to stop in

Sturgis to look around and get a T-shirt. However, we ended up returning two more times to complete the purchase of a leather jacket containing an air-brushed picture of a polar bear that Jane so desperately wanted.

When we were at Custer State Park, we were surprised when we encountered a herd of 500 buffalo grazing across the road in front of our motorcycles. We were told to give them all the room they wanted. This is especially true when you're riding a vulnerable motorcycle. We were also trying to stop to take close-up pictures while snorting, stomping, 7-foot-tall, 2,000-pound buffalo were just 30 feet in front and on both sides of us.

Having survived the encounter, we pressed on into Wyoming heading for Cody. We stopped at Devil's Tower, where we met other motorcyclists from all over. One group from Hawaii met us at the foot of the Tower. They had shipped their bikes over from Hawaii and were near the end of their trip after covering a western loop.

Wyoming was breathtaking and more beautiful than we had ever imagined. We spent six days at or near the rally site in Cody including jaunts to Yellowstone National Park just 52 miles away.

On the last day in Cody, we decided to take a short trip to Beartooth Pass. When we were 10 miles out of Cody, we were stopped by a flag person directing traffic in a road construction area. Two vehicles were in front of me, and Jane was behind me. When it came our turn, the vehicles in front of me started up and we followed. Within 100 yards I knew we had done something wrong.

My bike was swerving all over the road, and I thought I was going to fall. By some miracle, I was able to get it stopped; but as I looked back, I could see that Jane was on the ground, and her motorcycle was on its side in the mud. I ran back up the road to help the construction crew who were attempting to upright the bike. Jane had been thrown from the machine across the mud and gravel and was covered from helmet to toe with oozing mud.

Jane seemed OK, protected from most of the possible human damage by her leather jacket and a full-face helmet. The bike was damaged but rideable. It took the better part of half an hour for me to get the two bikes back up the road and clean off the mud caked on both the wheels and Jane. The road construction supervisor said, "You can thank that guy from Texas, who led you down the wrong road."

Jane felt better the next day, and we rode 300 miles back through Yellowstone and down to the Grand Teton Mountains. Jane's goal had finally been realized. We suffered through a downpour in Yellowstone on the way back to Cody. Jane was afraid that we'd have to pass through the high mountain region of Yellowstone where you ride next to the 3000-foot cliffs without guardrails. Fortunately, the rain stopped before we got to the bad area, so the trip back to Cody was uneventful albeit windy and cold.

Now, it was time to make the trip back to New Jersey. Warren decided that he would head back East using a southern route. Jane and I would start back over the 2,500 miles to New Jersey, alone.

We stopped in Minden, Nebraska, to visit Harold Warp's Pioneer Village. This museum contained numerous collections of automobiles, clothes, furniture, etc., arranged chronologically depicting the development of the United States.

We also stopped in Amana, Iowa, where the famous colonies are located. We had phoned ahead for a reservation in the motel there; but as we entered the town, we found the road blocked and no directions on how to get around it.

I rode around like an idiot for a while with Jane close behind. Finally, we backtracked to the place where the road was blocked, and I got off the bike to speak to a highway construction person sitting in a truck.

She told me to follow the signs back 6 miles to South Amana. Then, we were to follow the detour signs around a slowly curving road back to Amana.

We rode through Upper South Amana, South Amana, West Amana, High Amana, Middle Amana, Little Amana, and finally Amana. If we had continued past Amana, we would have come to East Amana.

Along the way, we passed by the plant where Amana appliances are made. We were told that the tourists were staying away this year owing to the flooding of the Iowa River.

At the Colony Inn Restaurant in Amana, our waitress, Marie, was especially noteworthy since she had the unusual talent of being able to read our minds, so we didn't need to tell her what we wanted.

She just sized us up and brought out our food without us having to utter a word.

When we got to Indianapolis, we encountered a severe thunderstorm. It was dark and windy, and the rain was pelting us. Lightning strikes were all around us. I pulled over under an overpass and ran back to where Jane had stopped. "I'm going to die out here," she cried hysterically. We agreed to pull ahead about a half mile to the next exit. We made it to the exit and sat in a McDonald's for over an hour waiting for the storm to subside. After that, we had no rain all the way home.

Jane was finding it more and more difficult to keep up with me on the trip back. She had received some bruises from her fall in Cody and these made travel by motorcycle difficult, but she persevered.

Finally, we crossed the bridge into New Jersey and headed north on the turnpike toward home. We were exhausted as we pulled into our driveway. The odometer showed we had covered nearly 6,000 miles in 24 days. Other than 30 minutes of rain through Yellowstone and the storm at Indianapolis, we had good weather all the way.

Well, it's past Labor Day now, and we just got through planning some Polar Bear Grand Tour rides. Jane said, "We have to think about getting a motel room in Lewes, Delaware."

I looked at her and replied, "Are you sure you want to go? I'm afraid someone will be there who will suggest that we join them on a ride to Alaska next year."

"Yeah," said Jane. "And you know what that means. You can go by yourself!"

While we were in Illinois, Jane's sister, Carol, told us how much she admired us for taking such a long trip on a first tour. Carol had taken quite a few trips by motorcycle, but all starting from Illinois. Thus, almost all her trips were within a thousand miles. She couldn't get over that we had traveled 2,500 miles to get to our destination.

I guess that it was something of an accomplishment for us; but for seasoned tourers, it would be considered nothing exceptional. We understand that and know that touring experiences are relative.

We hope that as the years go on, we will be able to make many more such trips and share more adventures. Maybe we won't make it to Alaska, but wherever we do end up, we expect to continue growing and having fun on our motorcycles.

38. That Dreaded Moment

Back to October 13, 1998

My thoughts of the past snapped back to the present when I heard the doorbell ring and saw my son, David, in the front door window. He had arrived to assist me in my bloodletting. The waiting was almost over. Though still nervous about what was going to happen next, I approached the door, unlocked the deadbolt, and let him in.

David, the oldest of the three children Jane and I were blessed with, is a handsome blond with exceptional talent as an actor, singer, and dancer. He did commercials and performed in Jersey Shore productions as well as regional theater. After attending the Mason Gross School of the Arts at Rutgers University, he pursued a career in dramatic arts and held various teaching positions.

We sat down on the couch near the wooden TV tray. (In fact, David had given Jane and me the set of TV trays one Christmas.) David wanted me to explain what this "test" was all about. I said, "It's a long story that will take a while to tell." He persisted in wanting me to elaborate.

I told him, "I think this test is going to drive me crazy. Why don't we get it over with first, and then we can have a Pepsi and talk."

"Sounds like a plan," he replied.

Then David reached for a lancet that he uses to test his sugar level. (As you may recall, David has had type 1 diabetes since he was 10 years old.) "Just hold your finger out and I'll do the rest," he said.

He proceeded to prick my finger with the lancet. Then he squeezed a few drops of my blood onto the clean cloth the researcher from Oxford University had sent me. "Now wasn't that easy?" he quipped.

"Thank God!" I rejoined, as I took a big breath and let it out.

"Now, what's the story here, Dad? Why are you doing this test?" asked David. "I've got the whole evening, so give."

"Well, it goes back to before my dad, your grandpa, died in 1992," I continued.

39. Jill's Notes

1988

In 1988 my brother, Ron, stopped by Dad's house in Normal to check on him and found Dad lying unconscious on the floor. Ron called the rescue squad, and they took Dad to the hospital. Doctors got him well enough to go home; however, after a couple of other incidents occurred, Ron and I agreed that he needed 24-hour care.

Dad was admitted to a nursing home that was only two blocks from his house. His hearing was good, but his eyesight was failing. His speech was somewhat slurred and at times incoherent. Nursing aids pushed him in a wheelchair to the dining hall for meals and social activities and provided any assistance he needed. (Ron and his wife, Carolyn, looked after his house and took care of his pet guinea pig.)

My sister, Kay, and her daughter, Jill, who was a student at Grand Canyon University (Phoenix), came to the nursing home from Arizona. Jill had not seen her grandpa for several years.

Our family knew little about Dad's past because he had never talked much about it; thus, Kay and Jill decided to record their conversations with him, hoping that they could get him to recall his boyhood in Indiana as well as his adult life before he married Mom.

Kay set up a microcassette recorder and asked Dad questions, while Jill listened intently and wrote his answers down in a notebook.

Before long, Dad was telling Kay and Jill about a harmonica he had won in a contest in Indiana when he was eight years old. He had taught himself how to play it. Playing tunes on his harmonica, he said, was one of the few pleasures he had while living with a stepfather who abused him.

Kay found a harmonica in a local store the next day and bought it for Dad. When she handed it to him, his gaunt face broke into a big smile. He put the instrument to his lips, took a breath, and began to blow softly into it. He had not forgotten the tunes he used to play!

Kay and Jill interviewed Dad for two more days and got the answers to questions that I had never even thought to ask.

During Dad's four years in the nursing home, he had a few minor strokes, and after the last one, he died on May 18, 1992, at the age of 84.

Buried in Jill's notes was a secret—one of many secrets yet to be uncovered. Here is what Jill found out from her grandpa. (I was able to obtain additional details from pantagraph.newspapers.com and other sources.)

About 1928

After Dad had returned to Indiana from California, he bought an auto repair garage in Bedford with money he had earned working in California. After a year he sold it and traveled to Bloomington, Illinois, with a friend who knew some people there. He got a job with Williams Oil-O-Matic.

One of Dad's friends introduced him to a young woman, Nellie Bly Moore. She was 19, and Dad was 22. They married in 1930 and lived on East Beecher Street in Bloomington. Nellie was soon pregnant.

I couldn't believe what I was reading in Jill's notes. I had to read it again. My dad had been *married* before? This was a giant secret that had never been divulged to my siblings or me. I could not even be sure that he had told my mom. She had never told me about his first marriage. Why? If the first wife was pregnant, did I have another sibling I knew nothing about?

Suddenly, I recalled something odd that Ron had mentioned to me once. Dad was asked to fill out admission papers at the nursing home. A staff member read the questions aloud to him, and he gave the answers verbally. One of the questions was "What is the name of your wife?" and Dad said, "Which one?" Could that have been the first hint that Mom was not Dad's only wife?

Perplexed, I continued to read.

One evening at midnight, Dad and Nellie were returning home from a card party. Dad was driving his Buick Roadster at 25 mph heading east on Locust Street in Bloomington. Suddenly, at the intersection with Roosevelt Avenue, a Buick Coupe (stolen in Peoria the previous week) driving north on Roosevelt, ran the stop sign at Locust and crashed into Dad's car.

The driver, John Short, and his companion, Lyle Barker, had been cruising around town waiting for the right time to rob a clothing store. They didn't know the town, and they didn't see the stop sign. They were criminals who had robbed a store in Peoria and then had driven to Bloomington looking for another store to rob. They were being chased by the police, who were right behind them.

In *The Daily Pantagraph* (March 30, 1931), Dad was quoted as saying, "Their automobile loomed up in front of me and I had no time to do anything."

Police officers were there in an instant, capturing the criminals and assisting with the crash victims. An ambulance transported Dad and his wife to Saint Joseph's Hospital. Nellie and her unborn child were dead on arrival. She had been thrown from the car and died almost instantly of skull fractures.

Dad was unconscious after the crash; but when police found him, he was holding Nellie, still in her fur coat, in his arms. His injuries (forehead lacerations and body cuts and bruises) kept him in the hospital for a week. Dad was devastated by the loss of Nellie and stayed with her family for a while before beginning a new path in his life.

John Short was convicted of manslaughter three months later and sent to Joliet (Illinois) Prison to serve an indeterminate one- to fourteen-year sentence. Lyle Barker got an indeterminate one- to ten-year term in the reformatory.

Now I know why Dad was so against my learning to drive a car when I was 16. He never, ever told me that he had lost both a wife (before Mom) and an unborn child in an automobile accident.

Dad met my mother, Margaret, three years later at a card game at the home of his friend, Johnnie Armstrong. According to Jill's notes, Dad said, "She was pretty and had brown hair. On our first date, we went to a picture show at the Irwin Theatre. Margaret liked me right off. She was my type." Eight months later, on September 15, 1934, they were married.

Mom and Dad lived in Bloomington on East Beecher Street, in the same house where Dad had lived with his first wife, Nellie. Did Dad tell my mother about his first wife and the car accident that had killed her and their unborn child? If he did, he must have sworn her to secrecy because she never uttered a word about these events to my siblings or to me for the remainder of her life. If he never told her, why was he so forthright in telling Kay and Jill when he was in the nursing home? These questions remain unanswered.

In 1940 Dad bought a house on South Linden Street in Normal for $3,500. I was two years old and Kay was a newborn. It would be the only house he ever owned.

While reading Jill's notes, Kay remembered a handwritten letter she had received from Raymond, Dad's half-brother, shortly after Dad died. At the time, something he said had puzzled her. She located the letter and reread it. On the first page, Raymond had written the following:

> "I'm glad I got to see Walter when we were able to talk to each other. I've visited Walter four or five

> times in the last 50 years, but he hasn't visited any of us in that time.
>
> Walter had a secret which he probably took to the grave. I think that's why he didn't come to visit. But none of us ever blamed him for what happened. It was an accident."

After reading Jill's notes, I still had many unanswered questions about Dad's life. I decided to go on the Internet and do some genealogical snooping. In fact, I got very interested in the subject of genealogy and started compiling charts of my ancestors. To help me out, my daughter, Susan, bought me genealogy software that I installed on my computer. That was the beginning of my search for the truth.

Jill's notes had said that Dad left home at the age of 18 and went to Bedford, Indiana, to live with his grandmother, Martha Elizabeth Fox Lyons Tannehill (Minnie's mother), and her daughters, Martha Elizabeth and Henrietta Tannehill. For the remainder of this memoir, I'll refer to my great-grandmother as Lizzie (her nickname), and my great-aunt, her daughter, as Martha to differentiate between the two Martha Elizabeths. Lizzie had two marriages. She married Thomas Lyons in 1887 when she was 17 years old. That marriage produced Minnie and her four brothers: Hovey, Daniel, Alvin, and John. After Thomas died in 1903, she married John Wesley Tannehill in 1906. That marriage produced Henrietta, Albert (Albert lived one day), and Martha.

I knew Martha's telephone number, so I called her one night in February 1998. She lived in Dayton, Ohio. She had been keeping some genealogical records also, which she sent me in the mail. She told me things I had never heard from either my mother or father.

At the age of three, Dad had gone to live with his stepfather, Earl Kern, when Dad's mother, Minnie, married Earl. That meant that my sainted grandmother was married before she became a Kern, or possibly, she wasn't married before at all.

Martha told me that Minnie had been married to another man, Lee Wesley Brown, at the age of 16. She had a stillborn child with him, and Brown deserted her. (I later found the desertion papers.) She then got a divorce from Brown, met another man, and had a child—my father—with him. Martha and the family were told that this other man's name was Harry Wright. This union, however, did not work out; and Wright married another woman shortly after Dad was born.

Minnie then married Earl Kern and took my dad to that marriage. Minnie had six additional children with Earl. "We believe that Walter was never adopted by Earl," Martha said, "but he started using the Kern surname."

In the nursing home, Dad had told Kay and Jill that his stepfather resented him, even spanked and beat him, but treated the other brothers and sisters kindly. It seemed that Dad had to bear the brunt of Earl's wrath because he was not Earl's biological child. (Martha would tell me soon the real reason.) Finally, Dad had enough of Earl's abuse and told Minnie that he was going to Bedford to live with his grandmother. Bedford was 10 miles from Williams, and Dad said he walked the distance.

Martha then revealed to me that my dad had accidentally killed his half-brother, Bart, with a shotgun when he was eight and Bart was three. I found a newspaper article (August 22, 1917) of this incident in a local Indiana newspaper. Here is an excerpt:

> "Bart Kern, the three-year-old son of Mr. and Mrs. Earl D. Kern, residing near the Stump Hole bridge, six miles west of the city, is dead as the result of a shot gun wound received Tuesday morning when a shot gun in the hands of his eight year old brother was accidentally discharged.

> The accident occurred at 9 o'clock Tuesday morning while the children were playing at the rear of the house.
>
> One was on the verandah at the rear of the house and the other was on some high ground about sixty feet away. The boy who was playing with the gun is about seven or eight years of age and could not tell anything of what happened. He had secured a loaded gun, however, and while playing with it the charge was exploded.
>
> The charge of shot took effect in the left side and back of the three year old boy. He lived until 3:30 o'clock Tuesday afternoon."

This was the secret that Dad's half-brother, Raymond, had written about to Kay in a handwritten letter, previously discussed.

After 20 years of marriage, Martha continued, Minnie became disillusioned with the marriage and left Earl. She got a divorce from Earl and married another man, Rollie Christenberry. They had one son, James.

Thus, my grandmother, Minnie, who I thought had only one marriage (to Earl Kern), actually had one marriage ending in divorce from Lee Wesley Brown (who deserted her), one liaison with Harry Wright, one failed marriage to Earl Kern, and one last marriage to Rollie Christenberry. Minnie had nine children (one stillborn) with four men. Dad was her oldest child. Again, we had never heard anything about this.

Martha sent me a picture purportedly of Harry Wright and my grandmother Minnie seated next to each other in a pose almost like an engagement photo. The man in the picture looked like my dad, even to the protruding ears.

I decided to do an Internet search for "Harry Wright" and was surprised when a link to a family tree led me directly to his name. After Harry left Minnie, he married Ermie Webb and had eight children with her.

I closely examined the ages of his children and found one son named Paul Wright, who was still alive and living in Anderson, Indiana.

I found his telephone number via Information, but I still did not know any way to prove that he and I were both related to Harry Wright. If we were, then I would know for sure that I was a long-lost member of the Wright family and that Harry Wright was my biological grandfather.

How could I prove that Paul Wright and I had Harry Wright as a common ancestor? Could my grandfather be the same as Paul's father?

April 15, 1998

It was just after 8 p.m. as I sat at my desk looking at the telephone number. Would this be the right Wright? Would he hang up on me as an Internet nut or would he welcome me, a stranger, into his family? Nothing ventured, nothing gained. I punched in Paul's number and waited for my answers.

The telephone was ringing. I was nervous. People don't like to be called about the past relationships of their fathers. I thought about hanging up but persisted until I heard a man's voice say "Hello" on the other end of the line.

"Hi," I replied. "My name is Walter Kern. Are you Paul Wright?"

"Yes I am," said the voice.

Gaining more courage, I continued. "You don't know me, but I found your name in a family tree on the Internet. It was the Girdley family tree."

"I remember that tree," replied Paul. "It has my whole family in it."

"Well, my dad died six years ago, and I spent some time talking to members of my family in Bedford that I'd never even seen before. They indicated that my dad might have been related to your dad, Harry Wright," I said.

"That might be true. I'm not sure. But I remember talk in my family about a possible situation where my dad and some woman might have had a relationship where a child was involved," said Paul. "It was before my mother and father were married."

"Well," I continued, "I'm just trying to see if Harry Wright might be my biological grandfather. I don't have any legal documents to back up this assertion. My dad never had a birth certificate. At least when he tried to apply for social security, he didn't have anything to backup that he was even born. That document might have existed somewhere, but he had no way to find it. He ended up having to sign some document affirming who he was and what his birthday was to get social security."

"I'm not sure what I can do. Perhaps I can ask around to my siblings to see if they know anything. Was there something specific you had in mind to ask me?" said Paul.

Paul and I continued talking for a while. I asked him a few questions and got some good answers in return. We agreed that Jane and I would make a trip to Anderson to meet with him and his wife soon.

It was becoming evident to me that I needed to travel to Indiana and do some more research.

Jane and I started out from New Jersey on May 4, 1998, and stayed with my great-aunt, Martha, in Dayton, Ohio, that night. The next day we drove to Anderson, Indiana, to visit with Paul and Anne Wright and stayed the night. Jane had already made arrangements to meet her sister, Carol, the next day in Anderson. She and Carol then drove back to Normal, Illinois, together, while I drove to Bedford and got a motel room for a few nights.

I wanted to visit the graves of my grandmother, Minnie, and her mother, my great-grandmother, Lizzie.

I first looked for the grave of Minnie Christenberry since she last was married to Rollie Christenberry. I got directions from her son, Raymond Kern, my dad's half-brother. (We were still using foldout maps in those days, and smartphones had not yet been invented.)

I was told that the cemetery was located on a gravel road that was off a main road. It was part of an existing farm. I was cautioned to be inconspicuous and not make too much noise because the farmer might come out to see what was going on.

I was traveling down a hill at 50 mph when I spied a tiny sign with the cemetery's name on it. I slammed on the brakes and made an abrupt left-hand turn onto the gravel road.

The individual gravel pieces I traveled on were large one-inch size and glistening white in color. I rumbled along with a cloud of white smoke behind me for about 200 yards, then saw the tiny cemetery and pulled in. There were no additional roads or paths inside the cemetery. I had to walk around from grave to grave looking for Minnie's gravestone. After about 5 minutes, I found the marker and the engraved name right next to the grave of her last husband, Rollie Christenberry.

It was lonely and quiet as I looked at the engravings. The graves were in the shade of a tree. My grandmother, Minnie, died in 1951 at the age of 61, when I was 13. She lived a short life and had nine children (one stillborn), three husbands, and other relationships including one that resulted in my dad's birth.

I next went to another (more accessible) cemetery in Bedford to look for the grave of my great-grandmother, Lizzie. The cemetery wasn't hard to find; however, it was a big cemetery with multiple internal roads and paths, and I was lost. I took out my cellphone and called my great-aunt, Martha, in Dayton. I told her where I was and tried to get directions from her as to where I should look. She had some difficulty explaining where the graves of her mother and father were. I walked around giving her landmarks and directions. I kept moving in a zig-zag path until I finally reached the plot.

My great-grandmother, Lizzie, died in 1960 at the age of 89, nine years after the death of my grandmother, Minnie. Lizzie had eight children (one boy living only one day), and two husbands. I was 22 and a senior in college and had never met my grandmother or my great-grandmother. I'm not sure why I felt I had to find their graves. I think I just wanted to see where they were and confirm the names and dates on the tombstones with my records.

I was fortunate to find and visit with Minnie's last child, Jim Christenberry. He had a large family of three sons and three daughters and lived in a remote trailer. He was a gregarious fellow, hard-working, and active. He showed me his family albums. I was thumbing through one that had his parents' wedding certificate, and I read out loud their wedding date. Suddenly, he realized that he had been born before that date and said, "I never knew that."

I met with Dad's half-brother, Raymond Kern, on his farm near Paragon, Indiana. I also sought out Dad's half-sister, Mary Cazee, at her home and spent a couple of hours with her. Mary had always been upset with her mother, Minnie, because she left Mary's father (Earl Kern) and all the Kern children. I was taking a video when she said to me, "What I can't understand is why Mother could walk off and leave all her kids and never want to check on them." Mary had never forgiven her mother.

I drove to Vincennes, Indiana, where Harry Wright had settled with his family. I had arranged to meet Ray and Doris in a parking lot. Doris was one of Harry Wright's granddaughters. I had previously kept in touch with Ray via email. He also kept an online database of Wright relatives that I had used. Ray and Doris lived in Olney, Illinois, known for its white squirrel population. When they arrived, I got in their car and they took me on a tour of Vincennes, where comedian Red Skelton was born and raised. (I videotaped much of the tour.)

I saw where Harry Wright had lived on a houseboat next to the Wabash River. I saw the place where Harry's father, Frank Wright, had a store. I saw the graves of Harry Wright and his wife, Ermie Webb, and the grave of Frank Wright. We crossed the Wabash into Illinois, at the same place where Abraham Lincoln had first crossed into Illinois. There was a monument there.

Then we went back across the Wabash into Vincennes, where I picked up my car. I followed Ray and Doris back to Olney where I stayed the night. The next day I drove the 160 miles north to Normal, where I joined Jane and Carol. The following day, we drove back to New Jersey, arriving May 11.

40. Y Chromosome

I remembered reading about a DNA study in 1998 that had been conducted to prove that Thomas Jefferson had fathered several children with one of his slaves, Sally Hemings. The study used the Y chromosome.

This sex-determining chromosome is present in males but not in females. Furthermore, the Y chromosome is passed from father to son mostly unchanged. A lightbulb went on when I thought about this. The Y chromosome passed from Harry Wright to my dad and then to me should be the same as the Y chromosome passed from Harry to his other son, Paul Wright. If I could test my Y chromosome with Paul's, they should match.

I called around to several DNA labs and found out that they were not doing Y chromosome studies yet. This was still experimental work being done by researchers in major universities in the United Kingdom and the United States. I was referred to Oxford University in England, where most of this work was being done. The DNA labs here could not give me any encouragement that anyone at Oxford would even be able to help me or what it might cost me. I guessed that it would be very expensive.

Not being deterred in my quest, on August 27, 1998, I sent an email to the Oxford researcher I had been referred to. One day later I received the following reply:

> Dear Walter,
>
> Thank you for your inquiry. Y chromosome DNA analysis can help you to some extent. If you and the potential relative you have identified have different types of Y chromosome, then you are not male-line relatives. If you both have the same type of Y chromosome, then you are likely to be male-line

> relatives, although this would not prove that the specific relationship you suspect is the correct one.
>
> We would be able to help you by analysing a set of Y markers called microsatellites that vary from chromosome to chromosome. We do not do this commercially and would not charge for the work. It would have to be fitted in when other work of the same kind was being carried out in the lab, so I cannot say how quickly it would be done. It could be weeks or a few months. We would want to be able to include the results, anonymously, along with other data from this lab. We would not want the results to be used in any legal situation.
>
> If you would like to go ahead, you need to send us the two samples.

Labor Day 1998 was coming up. I called Dad's half-brother, Raymond, who lived in Paragon, Indiana. I told him I wanted to meet with him and learn more about my Kern relatives. He suggested that both Jane and I come to the annual Kern reunion that was held on his farm. The reunion was to be Sunday, September 6. I had already been invited by Ray and Doris to attend the Wright reunion on September 13 in Illinois just across the Wabash River from Vincennes, Indiana. Jane wanted to spend a week with her sister in Normal. We decided to attend the Kern reunion together and then drive to Normal. I would then drive to Bedford alone for a few days to do family research. Then I would attend the Wright reunion in southern Illinois by myself. After the Wright reunion, I would return to Normal to pick up Jane for the return trip to New Jersey.

September 5, 1998

Jane and I drove from New Jersey headed for Illinois. As usual, we stopped in Dayton, Ohio, to see great-aunt Martha and stay over.

The next day we drove to Indiana, where we met many of my Kern relatives at the annual Kern reunion on Raymond Kern's expansive farm in Paragon (about 50 miles north of Bedford). I had begun to realize that all these Kerns were descendants of my grandmother and had the Kern line in them, but I didn't. Their Germanic roots were not my roots. My father's line was half from Minnie's line and half from Harry Wright's line. I needed to find my other family, the Wrights.

When we got to Normal, I spent a day there and then drove back to Bedford (about 250 miles).

I got a motel in Bedford and started looking around.

41. Birth Certificate

September 9, 1998

I still wished that I could find Dad's birth certificate. It had to be somewhere. All births had to be recorded with the county within 30 days so someone must have done that. Bedford would be the place to find it, if it existed. That was my next stop.

Bedford is the county seat of Lawrence County, Indiana. I had read that all birth and death records were available beginning with the year 1882. All the records were in the Health Department, and each genealogy search of these records cost $5. My dad must have inquired here to get his birth record when he was applying for social security, but they couldn't find his record. Consequently, I was ready for disappointment as I walked in the front door of the Lawrence County Health Department at 2419 Mitchell Road on September 9, 1998.

There was no one waiting as I walked up to the counter and made my request to a clerk. The clerk took me to where the birth record books were stored and said to take as much time as I needed to do a manual search. If I could find the record, they would type up an official copy for me. I was left alone to do my search.

I don't recall exactly how the books of birth records were organized. I know that I had to look through many heavy-bound books to find the names that I tried. I looked up Walter Lyons. No matches. I looked up Walter Kern. No matches. I looked up Walter Frederick Kern. No matches. I looked up Walter Wright. No matches. I looked up Walter Frederick Wright. No matches. I was getting pretty discouraged. Then I thought I would just look up the name Wright. There were many Wrights. Associated with each Wright name was a birth record containing first name, the name of the mother, the name of the father, and the name of the person who filed the report of birth. After about 30 minutes of searching, I found an unusual combination of facts that revealed a new secret.

There it was:

Mother's Name: Minnie Brown Lyons - Correct.

Date of Birth: March 25, 1908 - My dad had been assuming it to be March 22, 1908

The Name of the Person Recording the Birth: Lizzie Tannehill - Yes, my great-grandmother.

The Name of Father: Henry Wright - It should have said Harry, but the original written record could have been misread.

Then came the reason why my dad had not been able to find his birth certificate.

Name: Freddie Wright.

Freddie Wright! Unbelievable! It turned out that Dad's real name was Frederick Walter Wright.

Dad wasn't aware that his last name was given to him as Wright. He just assumed it was Lyons like his mother's.

He joined the Kern family at the age of three and started using the surname of his stepfather, Kern, but Dad was never adopted.

Dad didn't like being called Frederick Walter, so he simply reversed the names to Walter Frederick.

Obviously, Dad's mother and grandmother knew what his birth name was, but apparently, kept it to themselves and other close family members. If Dad knew, he evidently forgot.

I got a copy of Dad's birth record. I also located and got copies of the wedding certificate of Minnie and Earl Kern, and the Dissolution of Marriage for Minnie and Lee Wesley Brown.

I was elated at my findings!

Then I returned to Normal. While in Normal, I decided to call Paul Wright a second time to make a special request.

I told Paul what I had uncovered in Bedford. He was happy that I had been able to tie our two families a little tighter together. Then I said to Paul, "I did have something to ask you that you may find a little strange and somewhat intrusive. Have you heard about the Thomas Jefferson study where researchers were trying to use a Y chromosome to prove that certain of his slaves may have descended from Jefferson?"

There was a momentary pause before Paul spoke. "Yes, I have. But how does that affect me?"

I continued, "It seems that the Y chromosome that is passed from father to son and on down the male line has certain unchanging characteristics in the same family. Researchers were able to test the Y chromosome of Jefferson and the Y chromosome from several generations of his slaves and found them to be almost identical. I have made a contact within that study group at Oxford University in England, and they are willing to do a free study of you and me to see if we are related to each other. If so, I will have found that Harry Wright was my grandfather as well as your father. Does that sound crazy to you?"

Paul replied, "Well, that was the last thing I ever expected to hear when I picked up the phone, but you seem sincere, and your story seems to fit what I have heard over the years so what do you have in mind? I'm willing to cooperate if this won't be too difficult."

"I was sent instructions from Oxford University," I explained. "You and I must each submit a blood sample. That's the intrusive part—"

Suddenly, Paul interrupted, "That's not a problem for me. I'm always giving blood samples for some of my ailments. I can easily do that if it will help to resolve this situation."

Relieved, I said, "That's really good to hear. I didn't expect that you would be so receptive to my request, Paul. I will send you what I have to carry out the test. We both have to send our samples to Oxford University within 15 days. They could take a couple of months or longer before they have results. It's a complex test with many steps. I'm glad we don't have to pay for this, and we get to be part of their study, too."

After talking to Paul, I decided to drive to the same intersection where Dad had his accident in 1931. I drove north on Roosevelt Avenue and stopped maybe 50 feet from the Stop sign at Locust Street. I just sat there in silence, deep in thought. I imagined that I was in the Buick Coupe with the robbers as they sped through the Stop sign, directly in the path of Dad's Buick. In that horrific crash, two lives were snuffed out, and my own life on this earth became a possibility. The events of a few seconds had changed the destiny of so many people.

On September 13, 1998, I drove south from Normal to a park in southern Illinois just across the Wabash River from Vincennes, Indiana, where I met all of my Wright relatives at the Wright reunion. Unbelievable to me, they welcomed me with open arms.

The Wright reunion was a yearly event. This year there was a new member of the Wright clan, me. However, Harry Wright, who had died September 5, 1949, at the age of 63, was still the most talked about name at the gathering. His children were getting on in age. They had families that had families. A new branch had been added to the Wright family tree. Dad was Harry Wright's first son. I was to find out that Harry knew that Minnie had a son, but he never believed that the son was his. Whatever the relationship had been between Minnie and him, Harry broke away and married Ermie Webb on September 6, 1908, five months after Dad was born.

Dad had three children. They all married. Ron had no children. Kay had two girls; one had a boy and a girl; the other had no children. I had three children, two boys and a girl, and seven grandchildren, five boys and two girls. That makes a total of 18 direct descendants of Harry Wright (including my dad). Eleven of the 18 were born with the Kern surname, a name that should have been Wright. Dad's name on his birth certificate was Freddie Wright.

Harry was the father of two sons with Ermie. One died at the age of one. Paul was the other. He was still alive. His existence gave me the one opportunity I had to use a Y chromosome study. Harry had six daughters including one who lived only for a day.

Six children survived and had families, most of which were represented at the Wright reunion. Several Wright sisters arrived with scrapbooks of pictures and other information. I brought with me all the information I had uncovered in my search.

My visit to the Wright reunion had been successful. I met many Wright family members. They seemed to welcome me. They even remarked that I greatly resembled Harry Wright as they remembered him. I even thought that Paul's son, Brad, resembled in many ways my brother, Ron.

I was given an eight-page booklet written by Frieda Bernice Wright, the first child of Harry Wright and Ermie Webb. It was an unpublished mini-memoir. (Freida Bernice had died less than two years previous to the reunion.) She related what she had remembered about her early life. Had Harry married my grandmother, Minnie, she and my dad would have possibly lived this same kind of life. Also, none of the people at this Wright reunion, including me, would ever have been born.

The following are short excerpts (unedited) from Freida Bernice's memoir, *My Life Story As I Remember It*:

My parents were Harry Wright and Ermie Webb. They were married on September 6, 1908. They had eight children. Myself, Frieda Webb, (this is the name on my birth certificate). Mom began calling me Bernice while I was very young. I've been Bernice ever since. I didn't know the difference until I sent for my birth certificate. I was born on July 14, 1909, somewhere in Lawrence county, Indiana. Dad worked in a stone quarry . . .

Those days the table was left with things on it and the spread was thrown over it. We had no way of keeping things until the next meal in the summer time . . .

Sometime after little Carl was born we moved to the White river and lived in a tent . . .

We were below a rock bluff. There was a kind of hole in it. I remember when a storm came, Mom would bundle us kids in quilts and put us in that hole. She would go back and help Dad hold the tent up. If you touched the tent anywhere, it would leak in that spot. A railroad went above the bluff. One day the fireman threw out some ashes, and caught the cornfield on fire several yards from our tent . . . Dad had started up the river on foot. When Mom saw the fire she began screaming for Dad. He heard and came back. I don't think we were in any danger, but Mom was always excitable . . .

I haven't said what or how Dad made a living. He and the others dragged the river for mussel shells . . .

One day the other families moved to Vincennes, Indiana. We moved also but to a tent on the banks of

> the Wabash River. Then we moved to a houseboat on the river . . .
>
> Our next move was up the hill from the boat into a one room shack on stilts . . . While there, Dad found a pearl . . . Well, Dad held on to that pearl until someone offered $450.00 for it . . . That pearl helped buy the house at the end of Portland Avenue . . . I went to school at Harrison school until old enough for high school. I went to high school one year. I got a work permit and went to work at a cigar factory. I don't remember how long I worked there . . . I married Eugene H. Munger on September 16, 1926.

I left the reunion and headed back north to Normal where I picked up Jane, and we started the trek back to New Jersey. I still needed to verify that Harry Wright was my grandfather. Paul needed to send his blood sample to Oxford University; and, more terrifying, I needed to give my blood sample and also send it to Oxford.

42. Y Chromosome Results

October 13, 1998

David was half asleep when I finished my story. Kids just don't care as much as older adults do when they start figuring out the family tree. David said, "Dad, you certainly have uncovered some deep family secrets that none of us was aware of. Please keep us all up-to-date on this and give us each a copy of the results when you get them." With that, David got up. We hugged as usual, and he left.

I was pretty sure that I knew who I was now, but I needed this Y chromosome study to confirm everything. I wrapped up the blood sample and put it in a mailing envelope addressed to Oxford University. I knew that Paul Wright had already mailed in his sample.

The two independent samples were mailed off to Oxford. They arrived on October 20, 1998. Now more waiting, this time for results.

Correspondence continued between the researcher at Oxford and me until the final results were made available on September 1, 1999, nearly 10 1/2 months later. They told me it would take time, but I never imagined that it would end up taking so long.

September 1, 1999

The final report from Oxford gave a table of results for nine quantitative factors for both Paul and me. All the values were exactly the same for the two of us. The researcher indicated that several of the nine loci were very variable in the general population. However, they were the same for us. Our Y chromosomes were identical proving that Harry Wright was both Paul's father and my grandfather.

I was ecstatic! Science had worked its magic and confirmed that I was not a Kern; I was a member of the Harry Wright family, as were my dad, my siblings, and all our descendants.

I informed my kids of the Y chromosome results.

As expected, my three kids, all adults now with families of their own, hammered me with, "You mean we're going to have to change our names?"

"No kids, my birth certificate lists me as Walter Frederick Kern, and that's what I'm sticking with. I just have some complicated genealogy to deal with now."

At this point in my life, I knew quite a bit about my past but much more needed to be done to fill in a few salient holes I had uncovered. I wasn't sure I would ever have time to continue the research, so I tabled it for a while.

43. New Careers

After I had found out who I was, I embarked on a new phase of my life: retirement. That had started three years before in 1996. I was to find out that retirement was going to push me into a new career (or two, or three).

1996

I retired from Bell Labs in 1996 with 35 years of service. This was at the time that the Bell System was breaking up. Bell Labs itself was splitting in many directions. A new company, Lucent, was created that included Bell Labs and other associated pieces. A high-level executive at AT&T was appointed to create Lucent. She soon left AT&T to become CEO of Hewlett-Packard (H-P). You might recognize her name. She was in the news during the 2016 presidential campaign. Of course, she was Carly Fiorina.

I had been told that a study was once done to find out what happened to male engineers after they retired. It concluded that most died within three years because all the work-related activity they had grown to love evaporated after retirement. These men just couldn't take the non-engineer life. I was determined not to be one of them.

I formed the WFK Software Services Co. after I became very interested in this new thing: the Internet.

First, I read many technical books about things like HyperText Markup Language (HTML) coding and building websites. I built my own simple website, one page. I learned more and started making websites for other people and companies.

1999

One day, after building a website for a client, I was working to place his site on the major search engines. Consider where I was in time. It was 1999, and Google was only one year old, having been founded on September 4, 1998. It was not a big player at that time. I came upon a search engine called the Mining Company. At least I thought it was a search engine. I looked at the Mining Company website and found that it was more than a search engine. (The term "Mining" implied that it would mine information from the Internet for you.) It did offer searches but only in specific subject areas. It had so-called Guides for each subject area, and the company was looking for a Cycles Guide. I read the description. What they were actually looking for was a Motorcycles Guide. I had been riding for 10 years and had a lot of knowledge about motorcycles. I also liked to write, and I knew HTML used to create websites. I applied.

I had to create a small website of three pages and write one long story about my subject area. I wrote a story that I still have on my site today. They liked the story and my site and offered me a job. It would be a part-time job, maybe 15 hours a week. I asked them to change the subject area name from Cycles to Motorcycles, and they agreed. I would get $100 per month and had to start building the site and contribute three articles each week at a minimum.

The very next day, they changed the name of the company from the Mining Company to About.com (and even later they dropped the dot com and just used the word About for their name). I was now the Motorcycles Guide at About.com (About), one of 800 sites under the About umbrella.

I was associated with About.com for seven and one-half years ending at the end of 2006. I had built a site that included hundreds of original motorcycle articles written by me. The site had more than 10,000 pages and four motorcycle forums. I was working nearly 80 hours a week and had one of the top sites. My compensation had risen significantly over the years as About.com kept coming up with new ways to make money. It passed some of that income to the Guides depending on how many page views each site was getting.

July 17, 1999

Onc of my early articles as the Motorcycles Guide was about motorcycle risk. It also had to do with hearing of the death of John F. Kennedy, Jr. and experiencing an accident that occurred in my home that same day. It's entitled, "An Element of Risk - In Life and On Motorcycles":

> On Saturday, July 17, 1999, I had gone through my usual morning routine of fixing breakfast for my wife, Jane, and myself. Usually, we have eggs. On this day, I decided that we had been eating too many eggs so I announced to my wife that I would make cereal for myself. She then usually fixes herself some instant pancakes. I had just got my cereal and was seated in the family room talking with Jane who was procrastinating getting her breakfast while she listened to me ramble on about nothing in particular.
>
> At almost precisely 8 a.m., I became conscious of a low steadily increasing roar like a freight train that was running right down the middle of our kitchen. I immediately jumped up thinking maybe our cat had toppled something over but it was way too loud for that. As I reached the door to the kitchen, I saw flying dishes sailing across the room as the overhead double-door cabinet that had stood faithfully for over 33 years over our center counter work surface, fell crashing into the middle of the floor in front of the sink exactly where I had stood just two minutes previously.
>
> The cabinet had been nailed to the wall with four large nails which somehow managed to stay anchored all these years up to that very instant. Broken dishes, cups, glasses, plates, teapots, coffee pots, and shot glasses were strewn all over the kitchen. I now know what the damage after a tornado must be like.

After the noise was over and our cat was permanently entrenched in the farthest corner of the living room in total shock, we began to survey the damage. We asked ourselves what would have happened if my wife had decided to get up and start fixing her breakfast instead of listening to me? What if our grandson had been playing on the floor when it fell? Frightening thoughts.

As we were starting to recover, we heard on the TV news that JFK, Jr's plane appeared to be lost near Martha's Vineyard. Another tragedy in the making for the Kennedy family.

The whole subject of risk comes to mind. I'm a motorcyclist. I should be used to risk. You can't be a rider without assuming some risk. Life is full of risk. JFK, Jr. assumed risk when he flew his plane under Visual Flight Rules through a foggy atmosphere under low light conditions. He appears to have been unable to manage the risks that surrounded him. I was unable to manage the risks that resulted in an aging kitchen cabinet finally falling away from a wall to potentially harm anyone in its path.

What can we do to manage risk in our daily lives? As motorcyclists, we owe it to ourselves and our loved ones to be aware that riding a motorcycle is risky.

I recently received an email from a reader requesting my advice as to whether he should let his young son take up off-road riding. Were there any statistics on the safety of these bikes that I could find to assist him in making the decision of whether he should allow his son to ride? Well, what can you say? I told him there is an element of risk in riding, but we have to manage it by training, wearing protective clothing, and receiving proper supervision. Then riding can be a beneficial experience for both parent and child.

Yes, we need to manage risk but how do we do it?

First off, we need to get trained in proper and safe riding techniques to maximize the probability that we will survive that next ride.

We need to dress properly. That means wearing protective clothing and a helmet whether the law says so or not. Don't ride your bike with a tank top, shorts, sneakers, and no gloves.

We need to ensure that our bikes are carefully maintained and roadworthy.

We need to ride under optimal conditions. We have all ridden in the rain. That's part of being a motorcyclist. We have all ridden at night, but many accidents occur at night. Nevertheless, we should try to minimize our risk of having an accident by avoiding these conditions where possible.

Don't ride at night, especially as you get older and your eyes aren't what they used to be.

Don't purposely start out riding in the rain or in the snow.

Don't ride after drinking or after taking medication that makes you drowsy.

There is an element of risk in motorcycling.

Here's a simple action plan to get you started in your general risk management education. First, I suggest that you walk to your kitchen and examine the mounting of your heaviest cabinets. There, you've done something positive to manage risk. Now, I want you to think about what positive steps you can take to manage your risks of motorcycling. You are not invincible as a rider. None of us are. JFK, Jr. wasn't invincible either. He just found himself in a risk situation that no one could manage.

Do your part to manage risk. There is an element of risk in motorcycling. Let's go manage it.

2003

About had asked its Automotive guides to each write an article to commemorate the long life of the Volkswagen Beetle since its final day of production was coming up. The following article was my contribution as the Motorcycles Guide. It covered my subject area and my life. I called it "Beetles and Bikes."

Part 1 - Before the Bike Bug

No man ever steps in the same river twice, for it's not the same river and he's not the same man.

-- Heraclitus (500 BC)

Not long ago I was walking through my family room on the way to my garage where I intended to check out my two motorcycle trikes for an upcoming trip. Just as I was about to open the door to the garage, I heard the TV blaring: "Volkswagen has just announced that it will be shutting down production of the Volkswagen Beetle at its Puebla, Mexico, plant later this summer." What? I knew that Volkswagen Beetles were no longer being sold in the

USA. In fact, I had owned a 1974 Volkswagen Beetle, and it was one of the last standard Beetles sold in this country. Soon after that, the VW Golf was introduced and then the Super Beetle was phased out. Competition and emission standards had taken their toll.

I reached the garage and stood there admiring my shiny red 2000 Honda Gold Wing 1500 SE with Motor Trike conversion.

It stood on the left side of my garage. Directly across from it was my wife's white 1998 Honda Gold Wing 1500 SE also with Motor Trike conversion. There were no cars in my garage these days, only these two trikes. I know something about last models too since my 2000 Gold Wing 1500 was the last model year for the 1500s before the Gold Wing 1800 was introduced in 2001.

I had lived in this house since 1966 and seen a succession of cars in this garage. I had raised three kids and helped with the raising of two of my five grandkids. The cars that lived in this garage had been a big part of that raising.

Motorcycles came into my life late, only 14 years ago. My last Volkswagen Beetle left this garage just two years before that. Maybe there was some part of me that missed the fun of owning a "people's car" and longed to have again a vehicle that brought spirit, independence, and freedom back into getting from point A to point B. Maybe that void ended up being filled by motorcycles. I don't know, but I'm sure it played a part.

I remember the first Volkswagen I owned. It was the first new car that my wife and I had ever purchased. We got married in 1961 and drove from Illinois to Massachusetts in a 1953 Chevy Belair 2-Door Hard Top. That car lasted only two years, and we wanted to get a new car. At the time we had one child on the way. I had seen all the cute ads for VWs that were everywhere and desperately wanted a Beetle. There was a shortage of some kind at the time, and people had to order a car and wait for it to be shipped from Wolfsburg, Germany. I kept calling the dealer weekly, but my car had not come in. Finally, after 75 days of waiting, I went to the dealer, and he said that it was hard to get a blue one as I wanted, but he had a couple of other colors in the back that I could have right away. One was a gray Bug with a sunroof. It was $1,750, more than I had wanted to pay, but I told him I'd take it.

That was the beginning of my love affair with the Beetle.

Part 2 - The Gray Bug

The 1963 Gray Bug was our first new car. We liked the rollback sunroof. When it was hot, just roll it back and let the hot air out. I lived just eight miles from work, and there was a hill I had to go up every morning. In the winter, this hill was often snow packed. At the bottom of the hill, I would start the Gray Bug moving at the traffic light and then slowly climb the hill all the way to the top without slipping the tires. Other drivers often couldn't make it or spun into the ditch.

I had a rotational assignment in Massachusetts for the summer, and we had to move up there into temporary quarters. Bcforc wc lcft, we took a trip home to Illinois to show off the baby. Then we rented a U-Haul trailer and pulled it up to Massachusetts with no problem.

Our son, who was one year old at the time, was placed in a car seat that was hooked over the rear seat. This was before mandatory seat belts or child restraints had even been thought of. On the trip back, we rented a different U-Haul. This one was bigger, and it was probably too much for the bug. You could hear the metal creaking as it pulled the trailer up hills. I was afraid the whole thing was coming apart.

We also took the Gray Bug home to Illinois at Thanksgiving once with two kids. We just put a piece of paneling over the backseat, covered it with a blanket and stuffed a few pillows around the outside. We put our suitcases in the window well and under the front hood (the trunk area) and plopped the kids in the seat. After a 2,000-mile round trip that included a snowstorm, we arrived back safely in New Jersey, but the car looked like a gray snowball.

The VW's sunroof was great for carrying long objects. We used it to transport our Christmas tree home. We saw other VW owners doing the same thing. It just had great utility.

When we began looking for our first house, we drove the Gray Bug all over Central Jersey with the two kids. Once, I decided to spend a Saturday going out on my own to look at houses, and because it was raining, I left the family at home. As I approached a particularly busy intersection, I became aware that the traffic ahead of me was stopping rapidly, and several collisions in front of me were occurring. I had almost stopped the Bug when I glanced in my rearview mirror and saw a huge Buick bearing down on me. It hit the Bug at 45 mph and apparently never saw me. The Bug was dead, crushed from both ends as the Buick pushed it into the car in front of me. I remember the seat flying backward pinning itself against the rear seat. If my kids had been in that seat, some serious leg damage might have occurred. My only visible injury was some blood seeping out under one of my thumbnails. I might have had some minor whiplash injury later. I learned that the cause of the accidents had been a fatal motorcycle crash a quarter mile ahead of me.

I went to the junkyard to see the Gray Bug one more time and wondered if I'd get another Bug someday.

Part 3 - The Blue Bug

Since our family was growing, we bought a 1965 Dodge Dart after the Gray Bug died. We had it about three years until my daughter was born, and we needed to get a second car. A friend at work had a 1960 Blue Bug that also had a sunroof. It ran well, so I bought it.

The sunroof was different from the one on the Gray Bug. This one had to be stretched backward and forward manually. The Blue Bug also didn't have a gas gauge. I put a strip of tape on the odometer and penciled in the mileage where we should begin looking for gas.

It did have a unique feature: a lever above the accelerator that controlled a reserve gas tank. If you were driving down the road and all of a sudden the engine started sputtering, you lifted your foot up and gave the lever a good kick. That opened the reserve tank, and the engine would come back to life in a few seconds.

One day I got a frantic call from my wife who had taken the car up to the grocery store. The car had stalled about a quarter of a mile from our house on a major highway. She couldn't get it going. She walked to the nearest phone and called me—this was way before cell phones. I got in the Dodge Dart and headed over to the spot where she was parked on the side of the road. I got in the Blue Bug, kicked the lever, and started the engine. It ran perfectly. My wife just couldn't get the technique of kicking that lever.

I think the only thing I did to the car other than a tune-up was a new set of tires. It ran flawlessly for two years. We decided to trade it in on a Chevy Station Wagon to accommodate our three kids. Somehow, the original owner of the Blue Bug heard we had traded it in and immediately called the dealer and bought it back. He may still be driving it.

Part 4 - The White Bug

When I sold the Dodge Dart, I bought a 1972 Fiat 128. It had a four-cylinder, water-cooled, front transverse-mounted engine with front-wheel drive. Unfortunately, people tried to warn me that Fiat technology was sometimes a game of chance. After two years of bad luck and numerous failures, I traded it in on a 1974 white VW Bug. I had to go back to technology I trusted.

The White Bug was a lot of fun, but it didn't have a sunroof—it was air-conditioned. A/C in a Beetle?

Yes, and it worked—sometimes. The engine seemed to complain a lot when the A/C was on. It's like it was trying to ask me, "Why didn't you get another sunroof?"

I used the White Bug for commuting for the first few years. Then my kids got older and started driving. Then one-by-one, each of my three kids learned how to drive a stick shift car by going out with me in the White Bug.

We spent many hours stalling the car and jerking through the gears trying to learn proper clutch action. Oh, and there were those trying times at the stop sign that was on an incline and heavy cross-traffic was coming in both directions. Each kid had to learn how to use the friction zone of the clutch to hold the car motionless and then dart forward quickly and smoothly when an opening occurred. I'm glad those days are over.

Two of my kids used the White Bug at college. Each had one or two accidents that added battle scars. The Bug was towed many times and spent a lot of time in the shop. I regularly took it to a mechanic who specialized in Beetles. He would go over the car with a fine-tooth comb every time I took it in. If I wanted five things done to it, he would convince me that it needed ten things to fix it properly.

Once, my son ran over a curb as he rounded a left-hand turn. That hurt the front axle severely. The White Bug was never the same after that. I had to replace the axle with a reconditioned axle. Then after six months or so the White Bug started complaining again. It made low groans in the front end on turns and dips in the road. Finally, as I was driving home after work one day, the whole front end collapsed with a giant shudder, and I limped home. The prospect of another front-axle replacement was more than my budget could bear. So, even though the White Bug still looked great both inside and out, its internals had given up the fight. I sold the White Bug for junk. That was 1987.

Just two years after that I began thinking about a Bug again. However, this time, it was the Motorcycle Bug. Since the VW Bug was gone from my life, I had replaced it with the Motorcycle Bug. I was hooked and would never be the same again.

Part 5 - The Bike Bug

In 1989, I went on a trip to my hometown in Illinois. After watching my nephew with his BMW motorcycle and seeing and talking to a Gold Wing rider at my motel on the way back to New Jersey, I knew that the Motorcycle Bug had struck. I turned to my wife and said, "I think it's time we both learned how to ride." She agreed and thus began a series of events and adventures leading to the creation of several motorcycle information websites. The first article I wrote on the old About.com Motorcycles site documented the beginnings of my motorcycle adventure.

My garage used to be filled with VW Bugs. I had them for a total of 17 years. Now my garage is filled with motorcycles. The one car I have left is sitting in the driveway. Much fun was had by my entire family as we drove the three Bugs.

They were part of the family. The kids are now married with families of their own. The three Bugs

> are gone too. All the millions of Bugs belonging to people all over the world will be gone in the next decade or two. No new ones will be built after this summer. Time is moving, technology is moving, and we will never step again into the same stream.
>
> For me, I have the memories of the Gray Bug, the Blue Bug, and the White Bug tied to my family life.
>
> Can the Motorcycle Bug survive for 17 years like my VW Bug ownership did? I hope so. One thing I'm certain about—I'm having just as much fun with motorcycles as I did with my VW cars.
>
> So, stick around. Read my daily Motorcycle Views Blog, subscribe to my Motorcycle Views Newsletter, and read and contribute to my Motorcycle Views Forum. We all have the Motorcycle Bug, and no one will be stopping production of that Bug anytime soon.

At some point, About was sold to the New York Times, and their people moved into the management structure and attempted to evolve About to fit what its customers now seemed to want. They were now hiring new Guides who had more professional credentials. They wanted people who had written books or who were well known in their fields. At that time, I was nearing 69 years old, and they wanted me to be out testing new motorcycles. I was long past performing that job assignment but was attempting to emphasize user tests of motorcycles. This was at a time when almost no one else was doing such a thing. I already had a successful feature where actual owners of the bikes would submit their own User Reviews. That was not enough. My management felt that we should be the experts and not depend on users to give us their opinions. Of course, today, everyone wants to read user reviews and comments that real people have before they purchase anything.

Near the end of 2006, I was given an assignment, and if I didn't do it to their satisfaction, I would be fired. I spent a good month working on it and thought I had done well. But, they said I didn't meet their standard, and they quickly shut me off from access to my site while they searched for a new Motorcycles Guide. My opinion is that it didn't matter how well I did on the test. They were going to bid me goodbye no matter what.

I was able to extract most of my original content from the site and use it to create my own site, Motorcycle Views, in early 2007.

I had a lot of fun building the About.com Motorcycles site. I learned a lot. I met or interacted with thousands of motorcycle enthusiasts. I was even instrumental in seeing a group of fifty or so members of my site create their own motorcycle rally and continue it every year since. I was able to attend the rally twice that is held in Maggie Valley, North Carolina. I even saw two weddings of forum members who corresponded with each other, then met, and decided to get married.

Some may wonder what motorcycles Jane and I rode in our travels together. Here is a list of all the bikes along with some descriptive information about each of them:

My first bike was a 1981 Honda CM400T. I bought it from a friend for $600. It had a windshield, crash bars, and ran well. Both my wife and I used it as a starter bike, and both took our motorcycle driver test on it.

My second bike was a 1991 Honda Nighthawk CB750. This was a new bike purchased from my local dealer. I rode the CM400T for maybe a year before I got the Nighthawk. The CM400T was eventually sold for $600, the same amount I paid for it.

My third bike was a 1990 Honda Pacific Coast (PC800). It was an 800cc machine with a shaft drive and rear enclosed lift up trunk, a unique motorcycle useful for any distance.

My fourth bike was a 1994 Harley-Davidson Sportster XLH1200. I was getting an urge to break the Honda habit and bought this from a friend. It vibrated a lot and made exhaust noise I didn't like. I sold it after a couple of years and went back to my Honda habit.

My fifth bike was a 1998 Honda Gold Wing 1500. Notice the progression in size. When I was a beginner, I never thought I would be able to handle a Gold Wing; but time and experience made the transition easy. I sold my PC800 to a friend in our motorcycle club.

My sixth bike was a 2000 Honda Gold Wing 1500. No, I didn't crash the 1998 Wing. I converted it to a trike for my wife.

My seventh bike was the conversion of the 2000 Gold Wing into a trike using a Motor Trike kit installed by a dealer in Pennsylvania.

Here is the bike history for my wife, Jane, who started in motorcycling at the same time I did:

Her first bike was a 1981 Honda CM400T. This is the same bike mentioned above.

Her second bike was a 1989 Honda Shadow VLX600 cruiser. This was a new bike purchased from our local dealer. She got the first new bike, while I continued to ride the CM400T for maybe a year.

Her third bike was a 1990 Honda Pacific Coast (PC800). I sold my Nighthawk and continued to ride her VLX600 until she was sure she liked the PC800. Then I traded the VLX600 in on a second 1990 Honda Pacific Coast for myself (see above). I bought and personally installed a CB radio on both PC800s so my wife and I could communicate.

Her fourth bike was a 1998 Honda Gold Wing trike. This is the trike I converted from my 1998 Gold Wing. Eventually, she sold her PC800 to a friend in another motorcycle club.

Lately, I had occasion to review the movie *Purple Rain* for my website, Motorcycle Views. The movie is about the life of Prince. You may be thinking, "What does that have to do with this memoir?" Well, it is about Prince but it also has to do with motorcycles; in particular, it has to do with my first motorcycle (described above).

Prince Rogers Nelson, Prince, was born on June 7, 1958, and died on April 21, 2016.

I watched a program on TV about Prince's life which said that Prince acted in the movie, *Purple Rain*, released in 1984. Of course, I knew that. What I didn't know was that he liked motorcycles and owned and rode a 1981 Honda CM400 automatic.

He rode his personal motorcycle in *Purple Rain*. It had a Craig Vetter fairing that was painted purple. Prince's symbol even appeared on the bike. The bike had a 2-speed transmission that did not require a clutch. The foot gearshift went down to first and up to neutral and then to the second speed, but no clutch was required.

Then I thought, "*Wait a minute, they said: 1981 Honda CM400.*" That struck a chord in me, and I realized that they were talking about *my* first bike.

My first motorcycle was a 1981 Honda CM400T. The T meant that it had a Tachometer whereas Prince's bike was a 1981 CM400A. The A meant it had an Automatic transmission. (This model was also called a Hondamatic.) That made me want to take a look at the *Purple Rain* movie just to see the Honda and compare it to mine. So, I used the On Demand feature on my cable system to watch the *Purple Rain* movie. Then I wrote the following motorcycle movie review:

> Have you ever gone to a movie and seen the main character suddenly come out of a building in riding apparel and walk over to a motorcycle and get on? Well, when that happens to me, I get a sudden desire

to sit up straighter in my seat and wait to see what happens when he or she rides the bike. If I'm lucky, there will be many more scenes of riding to come. If I am exceptionally lucky, the motorcycle will become a major part of the story. Such was the case for me when I watched *Purple Rain*.

Maybe seeing a character riding a motorcycle in a movie doesn't affect other people as much as it does me; but, maybe the same thing happens to you, my riding friend.

Perhaps my interest was greatly increased because Prince's bike was almost identical to my starter bike.

I bought my 1981 Honda CM400T in 1989. It was a used bike and cost me $600. I've written about that bike on my site and in my newsletters.

The major difference between the appearance of Prince's motorcycle and mine was the Vetter fairing on Prince's bike. I just had a simple windscreen. Operationally, Prince's bike had a 2-speed, no-clutch, automatic transmission. Mine had a standard 5-speed manual transmission with a clutch.

Also, in the film, at least two other 1981 Honda CM400 bikes were outfitted to look the same as Prince's automatic except they were standard 5-speed manual transmission models (like mine). These bikes were ridden by stunt riders.

I counted at least a dozen times that the bike was featured in the movie. Once, Prince and Apollonia (his love interest) got on the bike and took a trip to a lake. There were closeups of her peering over his shoulder as he rode along. They spent time at the lake where she implored him to help her with her career. He told her that she needed to purify herself in the lake to pass initiation. She stripped naked to the waist and jumped into the icy water. All the time she was getting ready to make the jump, he was trying to get her to stop. When she emerged from the lake dripping wet and cold, he told her that she had jumped into the wrong lake. They had a small dispute and Prince ran to his bike, started it up, and quickly took off over the hill leaving her behind. But, he reconsidered and returned to get her on the bike, and they traveled home together.

There were scenes of Prince riding the bike back home, riding through city streets, and riding through the countryside, as well as scenes of Apollonia and him riding together.

There was a scene where Apollonia and her new boyfriend, Morris (Prince's competitor in music and with Apollonia), were arguing in an alley when Prince rode to the rescue, knocking down Morris with his bike. He then spun the bike around and headed back up the alley. Prince suddenly turned the bike around again and sped back to her yelling, "Get on." Then they sped off together on the motorcycle.

In between the beautifully shot motorcycle scenes, Prince sang many of his songs, danced a lot, got in competition with Morris, saw his mother and father fighting a lot, witnessed his dad trying to commit suicide, and saw his career fall on hard times only to eventually gain increased popularity, recognition, and success.

I learned that there were only three professional actors in the movie. The rest were real people who used their real names and performed in real bands in real clubs.

I was disappointed that nowhere did the bike get recognized for its superb performance in the movie. I wanted to see my first motorcycle get an award of some kind. I did find out that the motorcycle had its fairing repainted black and was then featured in the movie *Graffiti Bridge*, the 1999 sequel to *Purple Rain.* It was then retired to Prince's Paisley Park Estate. I'm sure it will be on display, so I guess it did win an award after all.

Well, I thought *Purple Rain* did a creditable job of advancing Prince's career. I thought his stage numbers were outstanding. His vocal range was not to be believed. I also thought he did a good job riding his bike back and forth across the screen enough times that all the memories of my first motorcycle came flooding back to me.

Thanks, Prince. Your music will live forever. You died way too soon. I'm just glad that you made movies such as *Purple Rain* and *Graffiti Bridge* and recorded so many albums that will allow future generations of fans to know you forever. Rest in Peace.

As Motorcycle Views grew, I began to wonder how long I would continue to run it. I knew the site held a lot of motorcycle information that would vanish if I closed it. Thus, I began thinking about writing a series of books that would capture some of that information forever, though I had no idea how to do that. In three years I would figure it out and find myself becoming an author.

44. Jane At 70

October 6, 2007

I wrote the following poem to my wife, Jane, and read it aloud at a 70th birthday celebration for her with our family. It relates many of the inventions that had occurred in her (and my) lifetime.

70 Years

To Jane,

The year was 1937. The month was October. The day was the 6th. It was the day that Jane Ann Cunning was born in Bloomington, Illinois.

1937 was a year like all years with important events and important people. It was the year that the Golden Gate Bridge was completed on the west coast and the Lincoln Tunnel opened on the east coast. The Hindenburg disaster occurred at Lakehurst, New Jersey, not too far from where we live right now in Freehold, New Jersey. *Look Magazine* started. Batman was introduced in Detective Comics and became the longest continuously published comic to the present time. Daffy Duck was introduced. The coronation of King George VI and Queen Elizabeth took place. Amelia Earhart was lost. JRR Tolkien's *The Hobbit* was first published. *Snow White and the Seven Dwarfs* became a full-length movie by Walt Disney.

Also born in 1937 were: Margaret O'Brien, Vanessa Redgrave, Suzanne Pleshette, Tommie Smothers, Roger Penske, Warren Beatty, Colin Powell, Jack Nicholson, Madeleine Albright, Morgan Freeman,

Dustin Hoffman, Robert Redford, Jane Fonda, Sir Anthony Hopkins, and Bill Cosby.

But so much for how things started and who your 1937 "classmates" were. They have all written their own stories. The following poem is about you. Your life story will have to wait a while longer.

Great Discoveries in Jane's Life:

Born in '37 the second daughter of Charlie and
Dorothy, she immediately was active and not just a
smidgeon.
Little did she know her movement would be
hastened by this year's invention of the jet engine.

Her future husband, Walt, born in '38 greeting the
world along with Teflon by golly.
Would take 21 years to meet her even though she
thought his name was Wally.

At the age of two, Jane was being tossed in the air
by her Papa, who never dropped her.
While the world moved on with a way to fly straight
up in a helicopter.

When she reached four, she watched the bees buzz
round her without any plan.
Even though people far away were building the first
aerosol spray can.

At her sixth birthday party, she played with some
brand new toys that some thought nutty.
But she had a ball anyway with her new slinky and
silly putty.

At the age of nine, it was just after World War II,
microwave ovens were just invented, but Jane had
no clue.

At age ten she didn't even know that the transistor
had been invented at Bell Laboratories,
or that her future husband, Walt, would be working
there, and she would be telling their kids stories.

At 17, Jane was an active high school junior who
cruised the Steak 'n Shake,
but McDonald's, new that year, their hamburgers
she could not take.

At 22, she met Walt at the Pantagraph. He had a '39
Chevy car.
That was the year the Barbie Doll came out. That's
lasted almost 50 years so far.

In '61, at 24, Jane and Walt wed and moved to MIT.
Valium came on the market. They might need it,
wait and see.

David was born in '62 when Jane was 25. He was to
become a singer.
Good thing the audio cassette came that year, his
music to bring her.

At 27, Jane gave birth to Steven. He was to become
a builder.
Permanent press came that year, another wonder to
bewilder.

At 29, Jane moved to her first and only house so far
in Freehold.
That was the year for electronic fuel injection, a
concept so bold.

Susan arrived when Jane was 30 and Taurus the
Bull was her sign.
Sue kept saying: I am not a bull! She wasn't lyin'.

As kids were raised from age 31 to 50, along came the computer mouse, floppy disk, MRI, space travel, cabbage patch kids doll, and laser printer, as well as the cell phone, Walkman, roller blades, Windows, liposuction and the Bic lighter.

Motorcycles were taken up at age 51 filling the void
from the empty nest.
Little did we know how our lives would change for
the best.

Walt retired in '96 when she was 59, but it only took
her one more year to retire.
She would end up helping raise two more kids but
not for hire.

At 60 she became a grandma (Nana) to Jordan, her
first grandson.
The world kept changing, but this was something
new and lots of fun.

At 61 she helped raise Connor, her second
grandson, during the day.
Walt helped too as he ran a Web site for About.com
to give his say.

At 63, she helped raise her Princess, Caroline, her
first granddaughter.
Caroline was smart and quick and sometimes did
things she hadn't oughter.

At 64, she had her third grandson, Jayson.
He quickly became Jay, a bundle of energy,
talkative and fun.

Her fourth grandson arrived when she was 66. Ian
was his name.
He loved his two brothers but sometimes gave them
the blame.

At 68, her second granddaughter, Andi Jaye, arrived
after already appearing on stage twice.
Her parents are theatrical, and now Andi takes the
stage on her own, so nice.

Now, at 70, Jane is barely getting her second wind.
After knee replacement, she's back for more.
70 is the new 50. With plenty of friends and
activities, she's always out the door.

70 years have come and gone. Where they went
could fill a book. Please write it, Hon.
Take a look at that smile, try to keep up with her
gait, and you know she's ready for 70 more years of
fun.

45. The Outer Banks

2008

Throughout our married life, Jane and I did a lot of things together. When our kids had left home, we took up motorcycling in 1989 and continued riding our own bikes together for nearly 18 years. In 2000 Jane switched to a 3-wheeled trike when her leg would not support her on two wheels. She was riding a red 1990 Honda Pacific Coast PC800 motorcycle at that time. I had been riding my white 1998 Honda Gold Wing 1500 SE for about a year and decided to have it converted to a trike for Jane. I then bought a red 2000 Honda Gold Wing 1500 SE for myself. My 1998 bike became her white 1998 Honda Gold Wing 1500 SE with Motor Trike Conversion. She loved that trike, after a few learning mishaps, and put nearly 50,000 miles on it.

Jane also had creative interests and consumed large amounts of time on the Internet, which led to going out to group sessions, writing to numerous people online, and making and receiving daily telephone calls. She joined several ceramics groups, participated in painting classes, made stained-glass projects, joined the Red Hat Society, the St. Peter's Churchwomen, the Saints Alive church adult group, the Spokes-Women Motorcycle Club, the Gold Wing Road Riders Association (GWRRA) Chapter F (F-Troup) riding group, the Polar Bear Grand Tour riding group, several scrapbooking groups (including at least one large group associated with the Scrapbooking site on About.com), the Cat's Meow group on the Internet, etc.

She also liked to pal around with several local women going on shopping trips, dinners, and even a few vacations in North Carolina at the Outer Banks. These were car trips. One such trip to the Outer Banks would prove a turning point in all our lives.

She and best girlfriends, Mary Ann and Diane, had gone for a week at the Outer Banks in North Carolina once or twice before. They had rented a house on the beach and driven down there with the car loaded with supplies and food. Once there, they would sightsee, go out to dinner, walk on the beach, and mainly relax and take it easy away from home.

These trips always energized Jane, and she returned home with even more energy that she could begin using with her various groups.

In 2008 they had planned another trip to the Outer Banks. They would start down on August 31 and return on September 6. This year was a little different. Our wedding anniversary would be September 2, and Jane almost didn't want to go since we would not be together on our 47th wedding anniversary. On August 30 she spent most of the day preparing for the trip including packing. That night we decided to go out to dinner at the Outback to celebrate our anniversary.

August 31, 2008

On August 31 Jane and I were both up early. We had a quick breakfast together as we always did with me cooking eggs for both of us. Mary Ann, who lived only two blocks from us, would be in our driveway at 6 a.m. packed and ready to go. Jane brought out all her travel bags and suitcases and placed them next to the front door. She was very nervous, but that was no different from all the other times we had gone on vacations together, or she and her girlfriends had taken their girls-only vacations. Being nervous was just the way she was. Once Jane got underway, she always calmed down and relaxed.

I kept getting up and down to peer out the three floor-to-ceiling windows in the living room, crouching down just enough to see under the roll-down blinds that had only been pulled down halfway. I did that maybe half a dozen times before Jane started saying how nervous she was. Maybe she shouldn't go. She would be missing our anniversary, and that was weighing heavily on her. She began a couple of extra trips to the bathroom as she waited. I tried to calm her down and ease her mind. This would be a trip she'd done before, and she always had fun at the Outer Banks. This would be no different.

She was worried about me more than usual. Two days before Jane left on her trip, she wrote an email to our son, Steven, with the subject: "Check on Dad." Here is that letter:

> August 29, 2008:
>
> Steven, I will be leaving Sunday at six a.m. to go to the Outer Banks with Mary Ann and Diane. Would you please check up with Dad most days? I will be gone until Sept 7. We will be married 47 years on Sept. 2. I am really hating leaving him. We have never been apart for our anniversary. Each morning the first thing I do is check to make sure he is okay.
>
> It was he that convinced me to go.
>
> He is fine. His health is good, but I still worry about him. I have been so blessed to have him these 47 years.
>
> We will go to the Outback tomorrow for dinner.
>
> Just call him, email him and make sure he is okay for me?
>
> I love you Dearly, Mom

On the morning of August 31, 2008, Mary Ann's car pulled up in the driveway, and I walked out with Jane, carrying her luggage. I put it on the floor of the back seat. I hugged her and kissed her and told her I loved her and to have a good time. She got in the car. The car backed out of the driveway and headed up Hibernia Way. They were headed over to Diane's and then they would be traveling down the New Jersey Turnpike, over the Delaware Memorial Bridge, and then winding through the Delaware and Maryland roads that connected with the roads in North Carolina. This was the beginning of another of Jane's journeys.

I watched Mary Ann's car turn left onto Andorra Terrace and disappear among the trees. I turned and walked back up the sidewalk in front of the house and stepped up on the front stoop. I opened the storm door, walked into the foyer, waited for the damper on the storm door to close the door, shut the heavy wooden front door, locked it, and then activated the deadbolt lock. It was now just 6 a.m.

My day continued as usual. I knew the trip down would last about four hours and that within an hour after that, she would be calling me to tell me she had arrived safely. I should be hearing from her by 11:30 a.m. Of course with Jane, you never knew.

I remember waiting up for her once when she had gone on a motorcycle trip with some motorcycle friends. She was supposed to be home by 6 p.m. I kept going out in the garage and standing in the opened garage doorway just waiting. I tried to call her cellphone but got no answer. I was getting panicky and almost ready to get on my motorcycle and go looking for her when I saw the headlight on her trike round the corner two blocks away and head toward me. She turned left at the corner and then did an immediate right into our driveway. She pulled straight ahead toward me and into the garage, braked, shut the ignition off, pulled her face shield up, swung her right leg over the seat, and approached me. "Hi, Honey. I'm home," she said.

"You're late. I've been waiting for you. I was just about ready to come looking for you," I replied.

"We decided to stop for ice cream!" she said enthusiastically.

That was Jane. She was just out having fun with her motorcycle friends.

I'm not sure what I did after Jane left on her trip. I must have straightened up the kitchen and then gone on the Internet awhile to work on my website—that's what I did a lot. I know it was around noontime when I came out and fixed myself a peanut butter and jelly sandwich and brewed an instant decaf coffee. I brought a paper plate containing the sandwich into the family room, placed it on a wooden TV tray, and switched on the TV. I don't think I had eaten more than two bites when I was conscious of noise outside, like a car door slamming.

I got up and walked to the dining room and peered out the window. A Freehold Township police car was parked at the curb just past the opening to my driveway. Two police officers were getting out of the car. One was walking up my driveway, while the other seemed to be walking in the direction of my next-door neighbor's house. I thought something was going on in the neighborhood, and the cops had come to check it out. I heard the doorbell ring a couple of times. I approached the door and unlocked it; and as I opened it, the police officer said, "Are you Walter Kern?" I said that I was. He continued, "Could you step back into the house. Is there anyone here with you?"

"I'm here by myself," I said. Just then, the other police officer arrived with Warren and Mary in tow. They lived next door and had been asked by the other police officer if they were good friends of mine. They had said yes and were then asked to accompany him so we could all talk together. The first police officer asked me to sit down in the family room so he could talk to me. I had no idea what was going on, but I began to get a sick feeling in my stomach. I recall saying, "I don't need to sit down. I'll stand. Now, what's going on? Tell me."

"I'm very sorry to tell you this Mr. Kern, but your wife Jane has been killed in an automobile accident in Pocomoke City, Maryland, at 10 a.m. this morning."

This was one of those times when your emotions get pushed to the background, and your mind tries to be rational. I wanted details. I said, "Arc you surc it was her? There were three people in the car. What about the others?"

The police officer paused for a few seconds and then continued, "From the report I got from the police down there, the driver of the car, Mary Ann, is in bad shape with multiple fractures. They had to cut her out of the car and take her to a Baltimore hospital. The lady in the back seat somehow got out of the car and was found dazed with minor injuries in a grassy area. The driver of the other car was dead on the scene. Your wife was in the right front seat with a seatbelt on but trapped by the force of the accident. She was unresponsive and had to be removed from the car. She did not survive."

My mind was racing with all these unbelievable facts having been thrown at me. I could see that my neighbors were visibly shaken knowing they had lost a treasured friend and neighbor in Jane. At the same time, they were offering their support to me. I asked the police officer, "How can I contact the police down there to get more details?"

"I have the name of the officer in charge and his telephone number. Call him. Talk to him. I've asked Warren and Mary to stay with you. We are willing to stay here with you also as long as you like. Do you want one or both of us to stay?"

I didn't want anyone to leave just yet. I asked everyone if they would all stay while I tried to get in touch with the Maryland police. They all agreed. I got on the phone and spoke to the officer in charge on the scene. He gave me more details and convinced me that Jane was the person who died in that car. They said that there is a diagonal access highway that crosses the road they were on that has double stop signs separating it from the main road. The driver of the car apparently did not see the stop signs and sped diagonally across the busy road right into Jane's car, spinning it around 180 degrees and stopping all traffic. The other car ended upside down in the center median on fire, and the driver died at the scene. It was all true. My wife of almost 47 years had died in a fiery crash 200 miles from home, and there had been nothing I could have done to save her. I felt I had let her down. I had not been there to help.

After I had gotten some more numbers to call and had confirmed all the information the police had in their accident report, I thanked the Maryland Police for their assistance and then told the Freehold Township Police that I had enough information for now. I thanked them all for what they had done for me and saw them out. I returned to the family room, where Warren and Mary sat waiting for me.

46. Sadness

Now, only Warren and Mary remained in the family room with me. As I picked up the phone, I told them, "Now comes the hardest and saddest part. I have to call my three kids and tell them."

Each call I made to my grown children was harder than the last. They were all in their early forties but had remained extremely close to their mother and me. I was surprised that I was able to reach each person on the first try. Each was deeply saddened and shocked. Some thought that she had been on her motorcycle—a persistent worry among family members that had never become a reality. Each promised to come down as quickly as possible.

Then I had to call her only sibling, her sister, Carol, in Normal. Carol had already lost her mother and father and then her beloved husband, Jack. To lose now her only sister, just five years younger than her, was almost too sad for words. She also said she would fly out to New Jersey.

Next, I had to call a representative from each of her organizations starting with our Gold Wing motorcycle chapter. I called Mike, who was the most gregarious member of the chapter and the most active. He was devastated. I could hear his wife crying in the background. That would be the case with everyone I called. Jane had been loved by everyone. She had no enemies, only friends.

There were to be many emails, phone calls, and forum postings to come. There were no Facebook posts since Jane had not yet become a member of Facebook.

This is a copy of an email I sent to one of Jane's many friends after they had sent her a normal email to start the day:

> Ralph & Suzie,
>
> Ralph, I am so sorry that I have to tell you this.

My beloved Jane has died in a terrible automobile crash in Maryland as she and two of her friends were en route to a 9-day vacation on the Outer Banks.

We had celebrated our 47th anniversary the night before and exchanged anniversary cards.

I helped her pack her friend's car for the trip the next day.

On Sunday, August 31, she got up early, and I was up with her since she was to leave at 5:50 a.m.

I went out to the car and stuffed her one remaining bag in the back seat.

I hugged her and kissed her and told her to have a good time.

She got in the front seat, shut the door and the car backed out of the drive onto the street. It turned and headed west as I waved good-bye.

They went to pick up their other friend who got in the left rear seat. The right rear seat was packed with luggage.

Jane had been asked by her friend who owned the car to drive the route down the New Jersey Turnpike, over the Delaware bridge and into Delaware, which she did.

They then changed drivers at some point, and Jane was now in the right front seat.

They were headed down Route 13 and had just passed the little town of Pocomoke City, Maryland when it happened.

The actual events are still unclear, but it appears that from out of nowhere another car approached their car on a collision course. The car Jane was riding in was struck by a massive impact somewhere in the front end.

The car that hit Jane ended up on its roof in the grassy median area. Fire broke out in the engine compartments of both cars. The rescue and fire people were on the scene quickly, and a massive effort was scaled to get the victims out. The driver was killed.

The driver of Jane's car was pulled out after a long effort. The friend in the rear seat was pulled out the window of the rear door by a passerby.

Jane's friend, the driver, is in the hospital with multiple leg, arm, and ankle fractures. Her other friend, in the back seat, has back fractures and is expected to be released soon.

Jane died at the scene.

God rest her soul.

Walt

The last words penned by Jane were found in her trip notebook returned to me in her personal effects:

> 8-31-08 5:50
>
> Mary Ann picks me up.

As anyone can attest to who has ever had to plan a funeral in the midst of extreme sorrow, there were seemingly millions of details to attend to. My kids helped immeasurably. Jane had one of the biggest funerals ever held in Freehold Township. Each one of her many organizations was there in force. I'm sure I made some mistakes but tried to minimize them. We had a cortège with me riding her white trike behind the funeral hearse going from the funeral home to St. Peter's Church in Freehold and then out to the gravesite at Old Tennent Church Cemetery, a few miles west of Freehold.

I'll never forget the wall of red shirts representing our Gold Wing Chapter F at the gravesite. All of Jane's three children and seven grandchildren (one still in the womb with a gestational age of six weeks) were there. Her trike was parked on the interior cemetery road, maybe 15 steps away from the gravesite. (She had recently told me that this trike would be her last motorcycle, but I hadn't believed her.)

January 2009

I needed to thank these members of F-Troup, and I also needed to write something about Jane. I decided to write an article for *Wing World Magazine*, the monthly publication of the GWRRA going out to more than 40,000 recipients. It's entitled: "She Didn't Fit the Mold So She Changed It."

> This is a story about my wife, Jane Ann Kern. Nine years ago, Jane and I joined Chapter NJ-F (F-Troop) of the Gold Wing Road Riders Association

(GWRRA). It proved to be our best motorcycle decision.

We had come into motorcycling late in life at the age of 51. A chance discussion with Jane's sister and brother-in-law, while we were on a trip to our hometown in Illinois, had focused our thinking toward motorcycles. Her sister and brother-in-law had been riding BMW motorcycles for quite some time and were active in BMW groups. Their two sons rode BMWs too.

On the trip back to New Jersey, I said to Jane, "If we're ever going to get into motorcycling, we need to do it now and do it right."

We had been living the life of "married singles" for a while, and we knew that we needed a common interest especially since the last of our three children had just graduated from college. As soon as we got back to New Jersey, we enrolled in a Motorcycle Safety Foundation (MSF) class and took it together.

Of course, our kids thought we were crazy. Our daughter, Sue, said, "Most parents worry about what their kids are doing. In this family, the kids worry about what the parents are doing."

Our first bike was a 1981 Honda CM400T. After we each had got our own motorcycle endorsement, we shopped at the local Honda dealer and found a 1989 Honda Shadow VLX600 for Jane. It was our first new motorcycle. I remember looking at the Gold Wings at the dealer, thinking I would never be able to ride something that big.

Jane immediately wanted some women friends to ride with. She was always the joiner and felt she could learn something new better by being with other people enjoying the same thing. We sought out women's riding groups and found the Spokes-Women Motorcycle Club, a group of 40 women from all walks of life. Jane joined the group, and I became an associate member. Shortly after that, I created a website for the Spokes-Women that still exists today.

Jane enjoyed going to the Spokes-Women meetings and rides and especially making each and every one of the women her dear friend. Besides being a joiner, Jane was also a friend maker. Her whole life was centered on being a friend to everyone and helping her friends as much as she could.

When I suggested that I'd like to join a winter riding group of 500 riders called the Polar Bear Grand Tour, I figured she wouldn't want to do that at all. Her first response was, "Oh yeah, where do I sign up?" Thus began more than 17 years of riding every Sunday throughout the winter. I also created a website for the Polar Bears that I continue to maintain.

After more than ten years of riding with these two groups, Jane wanted more. She wanted to be in a group that was couple-oriented. One of our close friends suggested that we visit Chapter NJ-F (F-Troop) of the GWRRA.

That did it. Jane was hooked and was now in her element. She couldn't get over how friendly F-Troop members were. However, she noticed that almost all the women rode behind their husbands as pillion riders and didn't ride themselves. She took that as a challenge to get more women in the chapter to ride their own bikes.

Jane had recently changed from a bike to a trike after her doctor suggested that she stop riding because of a leg problem. I had purchased a new white 1998 Gold Wing bike, and I decided to have it converted to a trike for her. Initially, she was reluctant to give up her bike, so I kept it for a while. The trike grew on her, and she became an excellent trike rider.

Jane then set about becoming good friends with every person in the group. When she visited other chapters, she made more friends. She attended rallies in the district, region, and at the national Wing Ding rally. She made even more friends.

However, making friends hadn't always been so easy for Jane. Her childhood medical problems had got in the way.

Jane had crossed eyes as a child. The other kids taunted her. After she had completed the second grade, she was hit in the head with a swing. The teachers in third grade noticed that she had forgotten most of what she'd learned in the first two years. So, she had to repeat the first and second grades and also receive remedial education with a special education teacher.

Part of that training involved staying at a farm over the summer where her teacher lived. Jane credits her teacher with giving her back her life.

Still, by then she was two years behind her original school mates and was the oldest kid in class. She found it increasingly more difficult to make friends.

But she kept at it, joined many groups, and slowly started making friends. Her constant smile and willingness to befriend anyone made her more popular. After that, she eventually had an operation to correct her eyes.

She was always a bit of a tomboy. Once she had a boy come over to her house on a motorcycle. Her mother quickly dispatched him. But Jane liked motorcycles. Little did she know that it would take 35 more years before she owned one herself.

The GWRRA motto of "Friends for Fun, Safety, and Knowledge" fit Jane to a T. Making friends and being a friend were what Jane did best. She was very safety conscious and took two trike training classes to sharpen her skills. She became a Master Tour Rider (Level 4). She participated in many chapter classes to gain more knowledge about GWRRA operations.

Still, FUN was the main ingredient that F-Troop supplied. She became the Sunshine Lady keeping track of all the birthdays and anniversaries. She was constantly posting on the chapter forum, Troop Talk. She became known as "No Rain Jane" after everyone realized that her presence at an activity seemed to keep all the bad weather away.

In 2006, Jane and I were asked to be the Chapter Couple. I was somewhat reluctant at first so Jane began a campaign of sweetness that finally convinced me that we should take this position. As one of our sons, Steven, said, "Mom thought she had just won the Miss America contest when she was made Couple of the Year with Dad."

But that was Jane. Everyone loved Jane and her antics. She achieved everything she always wanted to do when she joined GWRRA. She convinced other women in the chapter that they could ride their own motorcycle too. Also, she convinced many to start riding trikes.

Most recently Jane and I held the Treasurer position for our chapter. 95 percent of the job was Jane's. I just checked what was going on and helped when a computer problem came up.

Jane had planned a car trip with two of her girlfriends to the Outer Banks of North Carolina. They had taken this trip before. I always let Jane go anywhere she wanted to (like I had a choice; she was fiercely independent).

On August 31, 2008, they left on their trip at 6 a.m. I saw them off. At 10 a.m. they were involved in a two-car accident in Pocomoke City, Maryland, and Jane lost her life. She was 70. Jane and the driver of the other car were both killed. The other two occupants of the car were still in the hospital or recovering at home more than five months later.

Jane was truly one-in-a-million. We were married for 47 years with the last 19 involved with motorcycles. The final nine years were mainly spent with Chapter NJ-F (F-Troop).

The Chapter Members rallied around me when Jane died and practically stopped whatever they were doing to aid my family of three children and six grandchildren and me. I owe a huge debt of gratitude to the entire GWRRA organization that also helped me immeasurably.

Jane had made friends everywhere. She had belonged to numerous other groups and made friends there as well. The visitation displayed the depth of her network of friends and "Jane stories" abounded. I was confronted with groups of her friends who all seemed to know more about my family and me from Jane's stories than I knew myself.

Jane had planned to walk in a 5K Walk to Cure Diabetes in September. She had already raised nearly $500 from online donations that supported the Juvenile Diabetes Research Foundation (JDRF). Both our son, David, and our granddaughter, Caroline, have type 1 diabetes.

After Jane's death, the donations and memorials poured in, many from GWRRA members. The final amount she raised was almost $3,600. Jane's family walked in her place.

I offer my heartfelt thanks to all GWRRA members for helping Jane to achieve her motorcycle goals. I'm sure that God is already finding new ways for her to make friends and have perpetual fun in her new heavenly life.

Jane loved GWRRA and all the people in it. "Friends for Fun, Safety, and Knowledge" is GWRRA's motto but it was Jane's too. She lived it her whole life.

47. Recovery

I received a lot of advice about bereavement. I was told to join a bereavement group. I joined two. One was actually in a building on the grounds of Old Tennent Church; the other was associated with the Centrastate Hospital in Freehold. (That hospital was founded as Freehold Area Hospital. We had pledged a yearly amount for three years to assist in its building. Our pledge was under the name of Jane's late father, Charles Cunning. His name is inscribed in the hospital somewhere.) I soon dropped out of the Centrastate group and concentrated on the group at Old Tennent Church.

I remember sitting in a circle with other people in grief counseling and being asked to "speak if you feel like it." Some had lost a child, others a sister or brother. Most had lost a husband or wife. We were cautioned not to make any big decisions in the first year. Don't sell your house. Don't get a new job. Don't look for a new partner. One woman had left the room of her dead son completely the same as it was when he died. Some of the mourners had seemed to be still sad after five or more years. Very few had moved on.

I had one evening of despair. I sat in my living room and prayed to God. Why had Jane been taken from me? I imagined over and over the horror that must have visited her as the accident occurred. I was told that she looked up and saw the other car coming right at her car and reacted by ducking down to her left over the center console. She had taken herself out of the area where the passenger airbag was to the uncertain position between the two airbags. I asked God for a sign that she was now OK. I prayed that she would visit me in a dream. That never happened. However, my neighbor, Warren, told me one day that he had a vivid dream about Jane. (Warren and his wife, Mary, had sat with me when I was visited by the two police officers from Freehold Township.) In his dream, Warren said, Jane was wearing a brightly colored sweater and thanked him for being there to help me when she died.

Within a day or two after the funeral, I was at home alone when I heard a distant dull roar from outside. I opened the sliding glass door in the family room and stepped out onto my wood deck. I moved as far away from the house as I could and scanned the sky. I could hear the sound more clearly, and I could see a dark cloud heading my way. It got closer and closer. A very large formation (a skein) of honking Canadian geese flew directly over my house.

This was not the usual skein one sees. It was big, a super skein of geese! The noise was deafening. I remembered reading in one of my bereavement books that some mourners had seen a similar formation after their loved ones had died. It was a sign from the departed that the mourners' loved ones were OK—a final goodbye in an attempt to relieve the mourners' pain of losing them. Was I personally serenaded by Jane's spirit being carried on one last trip past her home of 42 years? I had seen such skeins before but never one so large, noisy, and close to the ground. It came from the east and flew directly over me. I watched this huge assemblage of birds, all honking over my head and heading toward the setting sun. As the skein got smaller and smaller, it shifted direction and flew south. I could see it heading west again, turning north, and making another left turn heading back toward my house. Believe it or not, it made a return trip over my house for a second set of goodbyes from Jane. Maybe she had forgotten something. Who knows. The skein got even larger and lower to the ground than before as it honked over my house, this time disappearing for good into the sunset. It was a sight and experience that I will never forget. Perhaps it was just a coincidence, but it seemed to have been meant just for me. After that, I watched the sky every night for a month and never saw another formation like it again.

48. New Life

After five months of these bereavement sessions, I decided that I needed to start seeking the rest of my life. I had had 47 wonderful years of marriage, and I was lonely, very lonely. I didn't like the single life. All my kids were adults with their own lives. I wasn't ready to forego possible happiness for a sad existence for the rest of my life. I had told my daughter after a month that I would give it six months and then I would try to find where God wanted me to go.

I longed for companionship. I know that I was acting pretty stupid and juvenile at times as my eyes started wandering everywhere in search of someone to spend the rest of my life with. I want to publicly apologize for my behavior toward certain women. I actually wrote notes to some and kept the drafts in my daily journal. As I go back over them now, I see with new eyes, heart, and mind how stupid I was acting. In bereavement sessions, we were told that such behavior would happen. We would act irrationally at times. We would make bad decisions. We might not want to take the time required to meet people and establish new relationships. We were warned that we might start crying without warning as certain things happened. This would be uncharted territory for us. The mind and heart have been so filled with love for, and experiences with, our departed spouse that we want to hurry up and get that good feeling back. No two mourners will act the same way, we were told. Just try to remain calm, let time pass slowly, and gradually allow yourself to reach out to others who can help you become a new person on a new path into the future.

Someone at a Gold Wing chapter meeting told me that her girlfriend was interested in motorcycle trikes and was looking for a motorcycle trike rider to date. I thought that was a pretty lame reason to meet someone, but I did agree to a blind date at a popular Italian restaurant. I showed up at the appointed hour to find out that the place was packed and extremely noisy. I couldn't find the woman anywhere, but I really didn't know what she looked like. I sat outside and observed people as they entered. I went inside and looked around for someone who was doing the same thing. Finally, I went up to a probable candidate and asked if she was waiting for Walter Kern. She was. We finally got a table in a side room that was packed with people who were all talking at once. I sat across from her, and we talked. I found myself doing too much of the talking. I also wasn't very interested in her. We parted, and I told her I would call her. I was sure that she was not my type, so I called her and told her that I didn't see a particular match and asked her opinion. She shared the same opinion.

I told my friend who had suggested this meeting, and she said, "Have you ever thought about online dating? I hear that there are some sites that have age restrictions so you can search for people in a certain age group that live a certain distance from you. I'd give it a try if I were you."

I soon started looking at senior dating sites and found one that interested me. I entered my preferences and out popped a list of women's names. I looked at their pictures and read their descriptions. I even did Google searches on some. I called a few but could tell by their voices that they wouldn't work out.

I did find one whose picture revealed an elegant lady standing behind a dining room chair. She was beautiful. I thought I would have no chance with her, but, she intrigued me so I decided to call her. She was soft-spoken and sounded as beautiful as her picture. I told her about my past and about Jane. She seemed like the polar opposite of Jane. That was good. I wasn't looking for a replacement. I was looking for someone I could spend the rest of my life with. We agreed to meet in a public place, the food court at Freehold Raceway Mall, on a Sunday night.

March 8, 2009

I hadn't realized that most of the teenagers hang out on Sunday night at the Freehold Raceway Mall. It was crowded and very noisy. We had agreed to meet at a particular area in the food court near the merry-go-round. I arrived with a picture in my head that I remembered from the dating site. I stood there looking around slowly amid all the chaos. Then I was aware that someone had moved up in front of me. It was the lovely lady I had seen in the picture. She was a beautiful woman, 5 feet 4 inches tall with blonde hair, a perfect woman, the woman of my dreams. She spoke to me, and she had the loveliest whispered speech I had ever heard. She was not Jane. She was the woman with whom I would spend the rest of my life. Her name was Rosemarie.

In Memoriam: Ronald J. Kern (1948-2017)

My brother, Ron, died before this memoir could be published. Ron read the mostly-complete memoir and offered his suggestions on its content. I had driven out to Normal from New Jersey for the 6oth reunion of my high school class. While there, I spent several hours with Ron and his wife, Carolyn, as they poured through family albums for pictures that I might be able to use for this memoir. Ron was not a well man. He had been through a series of medical problems and still had an optimistic outlook on life that most people wouldn't have in the same situation. His problems had been identified and doctors and specialists assigned to work with him. Four months after I saw Ron for the last time, he was getting into his car to go to a follow-up consultation with his doctors when he suddenly slumped over, leaving us. He was 68 years old.

As I related in the memoir, Ron was 10 years younger than me. When he was a child, I worried that he would play on the Illinois Central train tracks and get injured. By the time I left for college, Ron was only 8. I didn't see much of him for the next five years except when I went to Illinois Wesleyan University for a year. When Ron was 13, I got married and left to go to MIT. I got home to Normal perhaps once every two years. Ron left for the Navy in 1970 and returned in 1972. He married Carolyn in 1975. I feel sad that I didn't share much of his life. After all, he was my only brother. One thing I know is that his personality never changed. He was always happy, and he and Carolyn were always happy. In many ways, he was much like our mother, Margaret. Ron and Mom are now together forever resting next to each other.

Pictures

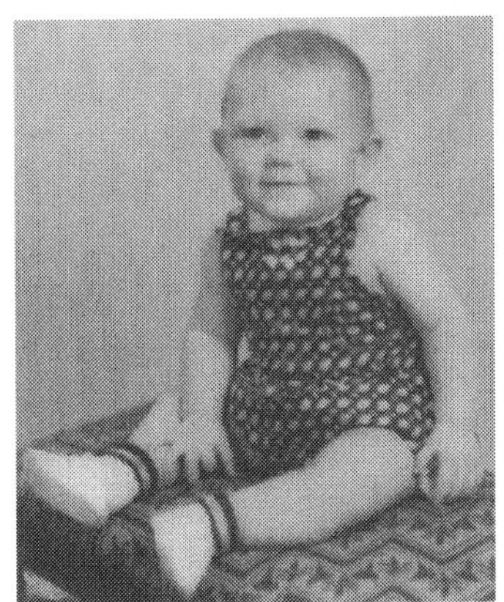

Me

Dad and Me

My House on Linden Street

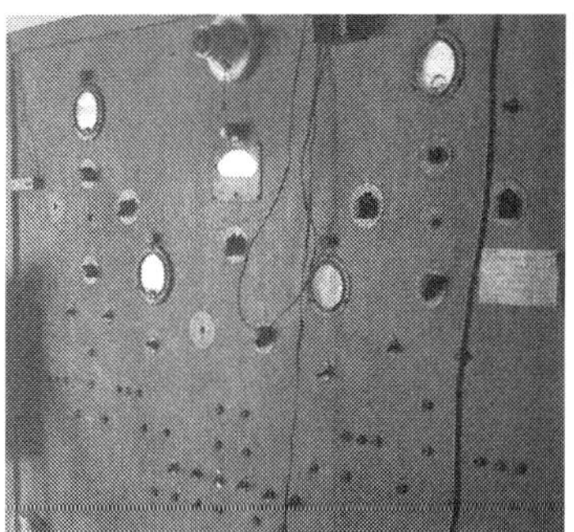

Dad's Electrical Board

Mom and Kay

Mom's "Darlings"

Me at 16

I'm driving my
1939 Chevy in 1956

Jane on her 1953
Chevy in August 1960

Jane and Walter on
MSM graduation day

Jane and Walter
at Uncle Watt's party

Wedding Party at
Uncle Watt's party
Jane, Walter, Kay,
Uncle Watt, Gayle and
Dave Owsley, Al

Wedding Picture: Charles and Dorothy Cunning,
Jane, Walter, Margaret and Walter Kern

1933 Chevrolet Town Sedan - Front

1933 Chevrolet Town Sedan - Side

Jill on bannister
in Linden Street home

Jill on dining room phone
in Linden Street home

Jill and Dad in nursing home

Paul Wright and I meet

Dad and Roadster

Dad and Nellie

Nellie Bly Moore

Harry Wright and Minnie Lee Lyons

Lizzie Dad

Me waving at the 1993 Sturgis Rally

Jane and I with our twin
1990 Honda PC800s

1963 Gray VW Sunroof

1960 Blue VW Sunroof

1974 White VW with A/C

Kitchen Cabinet Failure: View 1

Kitchen Cabinet Failure: View 2

Me on my 1981 Honda CM400T

Me on my 1991 Honda
Nighthawk CB750

My 1990 Honda PC800

My 1994 Harley-Davidson
Sportster XLH1200

Me on my 1998 Honda
Gold Wing GL1500

My 2000 Honda
Gold Wing GL1500

Me on my 2000 Honda
Gold Wing GL1500 Trike

Jane's 1981 Honda CM400T

Jane's 1989 Honda Shadow VLX600

Jane with her 1990 Honda PC800

Jane with her 1998 Honda
Gold Wing GL1500 Trike

Steven, Dad, Mom, Susan, and David

Dad

Jane and I brave the rain
at a rally in North Carolina

Rosemarie

Acknowledgments

I would like to acknowledge and thank my daughter, Susan Carol McKenna, who always stepped in at particular points in my life and pointed me in a new and beneficial direction.

Also, Rosemarie Dutka, Carol Aldridge, Ronald Kern, David Kern, Susan McKenna, and Steven Kern were quite helpful in reading the manuscript after it was mostly complete.

Marlene Kay Maloney, my sister, and an accomplished professional editor, assisted in the final editing. She also helped me remember details of our growing up together in Normal, Illinois.

I would also like to thank the online resource, pantagraph.newspapers.com, that afforded me research facts about Bloomington and Normal. My memory over the first 70 years of my life was surprisingly fresh and accurate in the writing of this memoir, but this resource was an indispensable aid in confirming certain dates and facts that were unclear to me.

I'd also like to thank selfpubbookcovers.com/RLSather for the excellent book cover design.

About the Author

Walter F. Kern spent 35 years as an electrical engineer for Bell Laboratories. After he had retired in 1996, he built websites for a while and then signed on at About.com as its Motorcycles Guide. There he started with a 3-page site and built it into one with more than 10,000 pages. After leaving About.com in 2007, he founded the Motorcycle Views website (motorcycleviews.com). He also manages the Polar Bear Grand Tour website (polarbeargrandtour.com) and takes all their weekly pictures in the winter. He took up motorcycling at the age of 51 together with his wife, Jane, who also rode her own motorcycle. Jane died in 2008 as a front seat passenger in an automobile accident. Walter currently lives in New Jersey with his fiancée, Rosemarie. He and Rosemarie are pet parents of a white nine-pound Maltipoo watchdog, Princee, and a white three-pound Maltipoo puppy, Coco. Most of Walter's writing is done at a winter home in Florida.

61897746R00153

Made in the USA
Lexington, KY
23 March 2017